BASKETBALL

The Skills of the Game

THE • SKILLS • OF • THE • GAME

BASKETBALL

Paul Stimpson
with Richard Taylor

The Crowood Press

First published in 1986 by
The Crowood Press Ltd
Ramsbury, Marlborough
Wiltshire SN8 2HR

Revised edition 1996
This impression 1999

British Library Cataloguing-in-Publication Data
A catalogue record for this book is available from the British Library.

ISBN 1 85223 986 7

Acknowledgements
Thanks go to the following:
Action photographs by Ian Christy.
Demonstration photographs by Mike Gibbons.
Author photograph by Sports Projects.

Line illustrations by Vanetta Joffe.

Photograph previous page: Players from both Worthing Bears and Manchester Giants
battle for a rebound at the 1995 Wembley play-offs.

Fonts used: text, Univers 55; headings, Univers 65 and Plantin Semi-bold

Typeset and designed by
D & N Publishing, Ramsbury, Marlborough, Wiltshire.

Printed by WBC Book Manufacturers, Mid Glamorgan.

Contents

Paul Stimpson, with over 120 senior international appearances for England and Great Britain, is one of the few 'home-grown' English players that consistently succeeded on the international basketball stage. He is a former England captain, and his 112 senior international caps for England is a record that has stood since 1988. He trained as a PE teacher and in 1984 became Director of the Crystal Palace Basketball School, which allowed him to travel around the country to schools and colleges coaching basketball wherever there was a demand. Paul is still heavily involved in basketball, marketing the game on an international level. He heads up the basketball department at ISL Marketing, the exclusive sports marketing partner to FIBA, the world governing body of basketball.

Richard Taylor is a freelance journalist specializing in basketball and has reported on the game from over twenty countries. He writes for national newspapers as well as for basketball publications.

During his career in English basketball Paul proved himself to be one of the best home-grown players ever. Not only has Paul still played more times for his country than anyone else, but he won a multitude of medals and cups during his club career.

Paul's technique was mastered, and skills developed, through hours of practice and dedication. This Skills of the Game book enables the basketball enthusiast to gain an insight into the philosophy of basketball and the skills and practices required to succeed in the sport.

Kevin Cadle – Britain's all-time most successful coach

Through his playing experience, combined with his teaching background and knowledge of international basketball, Paul is in a unique position to help any player or coach to improve his skills and understanding of basketball. In this book all of the principal skills required for playing and coaching the game are clearly explained and illustrated along with various practices that can be used to improve, both on an individual and a team level.

Michael Bett – twice English Coach of the Year

Introduction

Welcome to basketball! I promise you a sport that is fast, exciting and demanding yet rewarding; and it is a sport for everyone, men or women of every size. You do not have to be tall to be a natural basketball player.

HISTORY

Basketball began over a hundred years ago in 1892 when an American lecturer, Dr James Naismith, devised a game for his students in a Massachusetts college. This involved throwing a ball into a basket suspended above the ground. From this rudimentary beginning evolved the game as we know it.

Today, basketball's international federation (FIBA) has 201 affiliated nations, each with their own domestic leagues. These nations also compete against each other at club and national level in events such as the Olympic Games, the World Championships and European Club Championships.

Although the sport is considered 'new' to England, 1996 marked the sixtieth anniversary of organized basketball in England. The year 1936 saw the foundation of the Basket Ball Association and the first National Championships, won by Hoylake YMCA, who beat London Polytechnic 32–31. In 1960, nine teams formed the first National League, but it was boycotted by the London clubs. The first televised game, between Doncaster and Nottingham, took place in 1963. By this time the National League was down to five teams, and in 1969 it failed when England and Scotland decided to form a knock-out competition.

The current National League system started in 1972 when six clubs competed in one division – Avenue (London), Bruno Roughcutters (Liverpool), Sutton (now Crystal Palace), Loughborough (now Leicester), Sheffield and the RAF. Avenue were the first champions. The National League now has over seventy clubs competing in men's, women's and junior men's (since 1977) competitions, and there are also competitions for cadet men and junior women. Since 1971, the climax to the season has been the Championship Final at Wembley (apart from a brief three-year break from 1988–91 when the venue moved to Birmingham), continuing the tradition of the championship game which began with Hoylake defeating London Poly back in 1936.

THE GAME

Basketball is an indoor game played by two teams, each consisting of ten players. Of these ten players only five from each team can be on the court, playing, at any one time.

Sideline

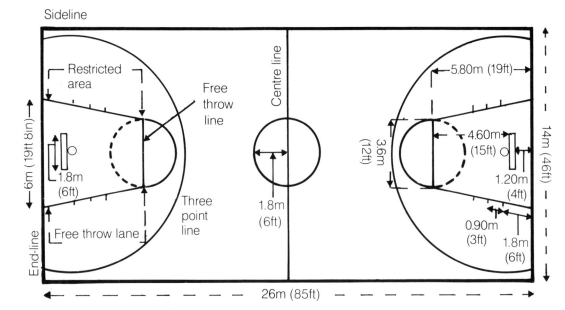

Fig 1   Dimensions of a basketball court. The height of the basket is 10ft (3m).

A full game lasts for forty minutes, and comprises either two halves of twenty minutes each or four quarters of ten minutes each. However, when the referee blows the whistle the electronically controlled clock stops, so that in fact a game will run for approximately one-and-a-quarter hours, including a half-time break.

Scoring

The idea of the game is simply to score more baskets and therefore more points than the other team. This can be done in a variety of ways. A normal shot is worth two points; penalty shots (free throws or foul shots) are worth only one point each as the player who is shooting has a completely free shot at the basket from 15ft (4.6m) away. The last type of shot is a long-range shot taken from behind an arc which is 22ft (6.7m) from the basket. This

is worth three points. As it is possible to score one, two or three points with a single shot, the lead can change sides with virtually every basket. When a team which is one point down scores with a normal field basket (worth two points) it goes into the lead by one point. With a long-range three-point shot a losing team can jump into the lead even if they are two points behind.

Time Limits

Another important factor which contributes to the thrill of the game is the set time limits. Once a team has the basketball and is attacking they have thirty seconds to take a shot. If the team does not take a shot within thirty seconds then the opposition is given possession.

When a team scores a basket, their opponents must pass the ball into court

8

from behind the end-line within five seconds. They then have ten seconds to move the ball over the half-way line. If they fail to do so the other team gains possession.

At each end of the court is an area around the basket in the shape of a keyhole, called the key or three-second area. No member of an attacking team can stay in this area for more than three seconds. If they do then the other team receives possession.

When a team has to put a ball in play either from the end-line or the sideline, they only have five seconds to pass the ball into the court. Failure to do so within this time limit results in the other team taking sideline possession.

Starting

The game starts at the beginning of each half (or quarter) with a jump ball at the centre circle. One player (either the tallest or the best jumper) from each team lines up on either side of the half-way line and the remainder of the players form around the centre circle. The referee throws the ball up between the two players, who then jump and try to tip the ball to one of their team-mates outside the circle.

Fouls

Basketball is termed a non-contact sport, but with ten players in such a small area contact is inevitable. Two officials (a referee and an umpire) control the game and call fouls on players when unfair contact occurs. When a foul is called on a player he must raise his hand. The referee then signals to the scorers' table the number of the player and the foul is noted against that player's number. Once a player has committed five fouls he

must leave the court and cannot take any further part in the game. The coach must then send on a replacement for the 'fouled-out' player.

Another aspect of the foul situation is that once a team has committed seven team fouls in a half, every further foul results in the other team shooting two foul shots. At the end of the first half the seven team fouls are cancelled, and the team foul count starts afresh at the beginning of the second half, although the fouls remain against the individual players.

Playing Positions

Now we come to the playing positions in basketball. There are three main positions: guards, forwards and centres (or posts).

GUARDS

Guards are usually the smaller, quicker players in a team. They must dribble the ball well as they control their team when attacking. They tend to play further away from the basket and so must be able to shoot from a longer distance than the other players. When a team has two guards on the court, one of them will often principally be a good ball-handler and passer while the other may be a good shooter.

FORWARDS

Forwards are generally taller than guards and tend to play on either side of the key. These players are good shooters, particularly from the sides of the key, and good passers, especially into the centres. Forwards are also expected to rebound much more than the guards as they are taller and play closer to the basket, and they therefore help the centres.

9

Fig 2   A two-handed dunk shot from Rebraca of Yugoslavia against France: one of the most exciting shots in basketball.

CENTRES

Centres (also posts or pivots) are the tallest players of the team and operate close to the basket (that is, around the key) where they can use their height to the best advantage. Centres are good shooters from close in and good rebounders; they also have to be good passers. These players are very important to a team as they score, rebound and use their size to intimidate the opposition. Sometimes centres are not the tallest players but are instead excellent jumpers and therefore effective in both shooting and rebounding.

Teams can use different line-ups of these players. For example, there can be two guards, two forwards and a centre; or one guard, two forwards and two centres.

Remember, basketball is a very fast-moving game involving five players in each team in a relatively small playing area. Therefore, teamwork, tactics, agility and fitness are very important.

All the players must be able to both attack and defend, thus they must be very versatile. It is the versatility demanded of them that makes basketball so appealing to the players. Everyone has to be able to do everything – shoot, pass, dribble, rebound and defend. In other sports the playing positions are much more specialized.

For spectators, basketball offers excitement as the scoreline is constantly changing. As the game is so fast-moving the coaches substitute the players in order to keep up the intensity of play. It is very hard for a player to play absolutely flat out both offensively and defensively for the whole game without taking a rest (being substituted). A player may get into foul trouble which means the coach must protect him so that he does not foul-out too early in the game.

The coach prepares and formulates his team's tactics – how they attack and defend. He is allowed two time-outs of one minute in each half for his team. Time-outs are an opportunity to change tactics or to reorganize the team.

It is impossible to have a tie in a basketball game, so if the two teams are tied at the end of forty minutes then five minutes overtime is played. All existing player and team fouls from the game continue into overtime and the coach is allowed one extra time-out. If there is still a tie, another five minutes of overtime is played, and so on until there is a result.

Captain's Role

Basketball is unusual among sports – certainly a great deal different from soccer or cricket, for example – in that the captain of a team may not have much influence during a match.

This is because only five players out of the team of ten can be on court at any one time. So, even if the captain is one of the best players on the team, he may spend quite a lot of time on the bench, especially if he quickly gets into foul trouble.

In basketball the coach decides the offence and the defence his team will play, and these instructions may be relayed to the players by the point guard as he brings the ball up the floor. The point guard will not necessarily be the captain.

The captain's role off the court and away from matches is to help build team

11

Fig 3   Cleave Lewis of the Worthing Bears looks for a way past the team defence of Trevor Gordon and Kevin St Kitts of the Manchester Giants.

morale and create an atmosphere of team spirit between the players. This will pull many teams through tough and close games.

KIT AND EQUIPMENT

When you start to play basketball, the equipment that you need is fairly basic and cheap compared with most other sports: a T-shirt or a singlet, a pair of shorts, socks and a pair of trainers.

As you become more interested in the game you may decide to invest in a pair of basketball boots as opposed to just trainers. Basketball boots are designed to protect your ankles, give comfort and provide a firm grip on the court while you are playing. Wear two pairs of socks when playing as this will reduce the chance of blisters. Make sure your boots fit well – they must be comfortable.

Some players wear basketball shoes (or low-cuts) as opposed to basketball boots (called high-cuts). Low-cuts come under the ankles whereas high-cuts go over the ankles. Personally, I prefer high-cuts as

Fig 4   Neville Austin of Thames Valley Tigers fakes his defender, Mark Harvey of Doncaster Panthers, before shooting the ball.

they give more protection and support to my ankles.

To practise on your own you will need your own basketball, the price of which could be anything from £10 upwards depending on the quality you want. When practising on your own you will be using your ball outside, so it is better to buy a rubber-covered one which will last much longer on all types of surface than a leather-covered ball (this should be reserved for indoor use).

FITNESS

There are a variety of exercises a young basketball player can use to loosen up, warm-up and generally stay in trim. Most of them can be done without equipment.

Skipping is a great aid to footwork as well as being an excellent exercise for strengthening the legs. It will also help nimbleness and quickness on the feet. Begin by trying to skip for a certain amount of time, or for a minimum number of skips. Then gradually build up stamina by increasing the time or the number. Skipping is very popular with a number of players as a warm-up routine before games.

Strength in the upper body can be improved through several simple exercises: press-ups build up the forearms and the wrists; sit-ups help the abdomen and stomach muscles in particular; and chest expanders are very good for strengthening the upper body and the arms. It is important to shoot after doing these exercises, firstly, to stop the muscles from becoming too tight and, very importantly,

to accustom you to shooting when tired. You will have to do this in the game, so, in practice, create a situation where you are tired when you have to shoot.

Sit-ups should be completed slowly; make the muscles work hard because that is how you will obtain the greatest benefit. Keep the soles of your feet flat on the floor and, very important, have the legs slightly bent. Do not try to do sit-ups with your legs flat on the ground as you can damage your back that way.

Jogging develops stamina. When you have the use of a court, sprint from the baseline to the foul-line and back; then to the half-way and back; then to the far foul-line and back; and finally to the other baseline and back.

Stepping up and down on a bottom stair will also build up the legs. Do this exercise for a short period of time initially and then build up.

Swimming is great for general fitness and exercise – and lovely during the close season in the summer!

Before a game, warm up properly. Slowly stretch the muscles in your legs, back and arms. Place one foot behind the other, then touch the toes on your front foot. In the hurdle stretch, sit down and place one leg out in front then pull the other foot back up to an angle of ninety degrees. Do the stretches slowly and steadily – don't pull a muscle before the big game!

This is a brief introduction to the game of basketball; the following chapters cover the basic skills and tactics of the game, and ways in which coaches and players can improve.

1
Ball Acquaintance

The starting point for a basketball player is to become used to the ball. The basketball is larger and heavier than those used in other team sports, games such as soccer, rugby and netball. Therefore, you must spend time becoming accustomed to the weight, size and feel of the basketball.

Drills

Just as in soccer, where young players kick the ball around and learn how to juggle with their feet, so in basketball there are drills and exercises to help you to 'get to know the ball'. These have two basic aims:

1. Complete control without dropping the ball.
2. Complete control without looking at the ball.

As you improve, you should aim to do the drills more quickly.

AROUND THE BODY
Holding the ball in your right hand, take it from the front of your waist to the back, pass it into your left hand, then bring the ball round to the front of your waist. Repeat this ten times. Then change direction, starting with the ball in your left hand in front of the waist, changing to the right hand behind your back, and bringing the ball round to the front of your waist. Repeat ten times.

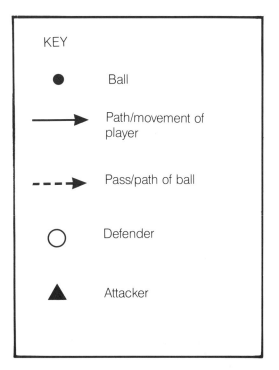

KEY

●   Ball

→   Path/movement of player

– – –▶   Pass/path of ball

○   Defender

▲   Attacker

Now repeat this same drill, but moving the ball under your armpits, then around your neck, your backside, your knees and your calves, then finally your ankles – *without looking at the ball*.

Now hold your arms straight above your head and tap the ball backwards and forwards between your hands using your fingertips. As you become more confident with the drills make sure you use your fingertips to control the ball, because they are what you will use

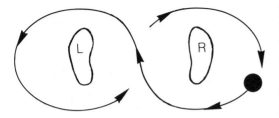

Fig 5   Thread the ball between the
legs in a figure-of-eight.

during a game. All of these drills are
designed to make your fingertips comfortable with the feel of the basketball.

FIGURE-OF-EIGHT *(Fig 5)*
Place your legs slightly more than
shoulder-width apart, then thread the ball
between your legs in a figure-of-eight.

Remember – your first aim is to avoid
dropping the ball and your second is to
avoid looking at it. Make sure you are
using your fingertips and swing into a
rhythm of moving the ball through your
legs. Move the ball ten times in one direction, then ten times in the other.

FIGURE-OF-EIGHT BEHIND THE BACK
Move the ball through one figure-of-eight
between your legs, then pass it once
round your waist before taking it down
into a repeat of the figure-of-eight, then
again behind your back, and so on.
Repeat ten times in one direction, then
ten times in the opposite direction.

TWO-HANDED BOUNCE
Stand with your feet shoulder-width
apart and hold the ball in two hands in
front of you. Bounce the ball backwards
through your legs to hit the floor level
with your heels. As the ball bounces up
behind you, move your hands quickly

into position behind your knees to catch
it. Now bounce the ball back through
your legs and move your hands back to
catch it in front this time.

This is a super drill for building your
confidence and co-ordination in handling
the ball. Again, concentrate on building a
rhythm without looking down at the ball.
Instead, try to look straight ahead all the
time. Build up speed and bounce the ball
harder.

TWO-HANDED OVERHEAD THROW
Hold the ball in both hands out in front
and throw it in a low arc back over your
head, then quickly put your hands behind
your back to catch it.

At first, throw the ball so that it just
clears your head, but as you become
more confident, throw it higher and higher. Of course, you will be unable to see the
ball as it drops behind you, so you must
move your hands and grasp it as soon as
it touches your fingertips. This drill is
excellent for developing a sixth sense for
the ball. *Remember – don't drop it.*

HAND SWITCH
Again, stand with the feet slightly more
than shoulder-width apart. Hold the ball
between your legs, but with the right
hand in front of the body and the left hand
behind the body. Let the ball drop
towards the floor from about knee height,
but, before it can bounce, switch the position of your hands (so that the left is in
front and the right hand behind the body)
and catch the ball before it hits the floor.

This is easy when you are looking
down at the ball – so don't! Keep your
eyes straight ahead and, as your confidence and co-ordination improve, build
up speed and gradually reduce the height
from which you drop the ball.

Fig 6   A penetrating dribble by Yugoslavia's Aleksander Djordjevic, one of the best guards in Europe.

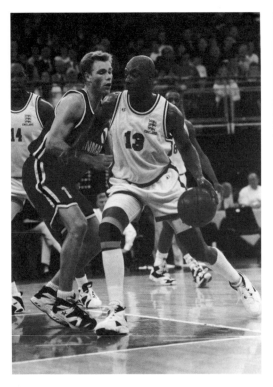

Fig 7   Steve Bucknell of England (and former Los Angeles Laker) dribbles past a Danish defender towards the basket. He is widely regarded as the best English player.

Fig 8   Toni Kukoc of Croatia and the Chicago Bulls dribbling the ball in the open court, always looking for a team-mate to pass to.

CRAB WALK

Stand with your left foot in front and the right placed behind, and hold the ball between your legs with the right hand to the front and the left hand behind the left leg. As you pass the ball through to your left hand, bring the right foot forward so that it is now the leading foot and take the ball in the left hand round in front of the left knee. Then pass the ball through your legs to the right hand, which is now placed behind the right knee. As your right hand touches the ball, take the left foot forward and then pass the ball back through the legs to the left hand again. Make sure that both feet are on the floor when passing the ball between your legs.

At every step, you are passing the ball between your legs without letting it touch the floor. As you improve, look ahead and build a faster and more confident rhythm.

2
Dribbling

Dribbling is probably the most natural skill involved in basketball. As soon as anyone is given the ball to play with, the first thing they want to do is bounce it. It looks easy, but there are many hours of practice ahead if you want to become an excellent dribbler. Dribbling is central to the game of basketball, so it is vital that you learn to dribble the ball correctly right from the start. When you are in possession in a game you will continue to dribble the ball until the moment you decide either to pass or shoot. So let's make sure you are always in control.

Technique

Of course, you use your hand to dribble the basketball and you can use only one hand at a time. But the palm of your hand never comes into contact with the ball. You dribble the ball with your finger pads, fingertips, or the top part of the fingers.

Never pat the ball. You should push with your arm and flick your wrist when bouncing the ball.

Never let the ball bounce higher than your waist when you are dribbling. The ball will usually be dribbled at a height between your waist and your knee.

You *must* be able to dribble the ball equally well with the left or right hand.

Never look down at the ball when you are dribbling. This is perhaps the biggest fault of basketball players.

Basketball is a team game and you will have four team-mates out on the floor with you. When you are dribbling you must be able to see them and your opponents, so that you can pass the ball immediately you see a team-mate in a better position than yourself. You will be unable to do that if you are looking at the ball instead of looking at them!

Individual Practice

PROTECTED DRIBBLE *(Figs 9 to 11)*
When you are dribbling close to a defender you must protect possession so that your opponent cannot 'steal' the ball from you. He will be trying very hard to do just that, because 'steals' are an important technique in basketball and some players specialize in robbing their opponents of the ball.

To protect the ball against the defender, keep it to your side away from the opponent and dribble it close to your foot on that side, with your knees bent. Drop your free shoulder – the one closest to the defender – and let your arm hang down to bar his way if he tries to reach in for the ball.

Remember – keep your head up so that you can watch the defender and also your team-mates.

If the defender makes a move for the ball, always keep your body between him and the ball. The ball must always be

Fig 9   Protected dribble: protect the ball by keeping it to the side away from the defender.

Fig 10   Drop your shoulder closest to the defender and let your free hand hang down to stop him reaching for the ball.

dribbled by the hand furthest from the defender.

ASSORTED DRIBBLES

1. Begin with the protected dribble, first with the right hand, then with the left.
2. Kneel down while dribbling the basketball, sit down and then lie back while still dribbling the ball. While on your back look up at the ceiling, not at the ball. This may sound an unlikely thing to happen in a game, but if you slip while in possession during a game you will have to keep on dribbling the ball, otherwise it will be given to your opponents.

   While you are lying down, you dribble the ball very close to the floor and this calls for a slightly different technique. Instead of flicking your wrist, you must keep the wrist firm and push with your finger pads.
3. After lying down, move back to the sitting position, still dribbling the ball without looking at it. Now dribble the ball towards your toes on the floor, then back to the hip and out at arm's length level with your shoulder. Bend your legs at the knee, dribble the ball under your knees to the other hand and repeat the drill with this hand.
4. Bend your legs a little more, then dribble the ball around the end of your toes to the other hand.

These excellent drills can be done anywhere as long as you have a basketball and a flat surface. The more you practise the easier the drills will become; and you will become a better ball handler – a fine asset to your team.

BOUNCE BALL FROM DEAD POSITION

Here is a simple drill which will greatly improve your 'feel' for the ball even though this is one situation which will not arise in the game.

In order to get the ball bouncing from a dead (stationary) position, hit it once, hard, with a loose wrist action. This will start the ball bouncing a little; as soon as this happens bounce the ball with a firm wrist, just as in the low, protected dribble.

DRIBBLING ON THE MOVE

When you are running and dribbling with the right hand, you bounce the ball slightly in front of you and to the side of your right foot. For a left-handed dribble, bounce the ball to the side and slightly in front of your left foot. So, as you run, the ball bounces to the side of your front foot. In this way you can move freely with the ball, or can quickly pick the ball up to shoot, pass or protect it from a defender.

Remember – when you are dribbling on the run always keep your head up and do not dribble the ball above waist height. Use your left hand if you are moving to the left and the right hand if you are moving to the right.

SPEED DRIBBLE *(Figs 12 to 15)*

In order to beat a defender on the dribble you may need a change of speed. In a full-speed dribble you push the basketball further out in front of your body because you will usually be dribbling into space, so you will not have to worry about protecting the ball. But always keep your head up and your eyes alert, ready to protect the ball if a defender moves in on you.

CHANGING HANDS

It is essential that you can dribble equally well with either hand – and there is no escaping that need. A one-handed dribbler is only half a player.

Fig 11   Excellent protected dribble by Sarunas Marciulionis of Lithuania whilst being put under pressure by his defensive player.

Fig 12   Mark Robinson of the Manchester Giants dribbling the ball at speed in the open court.

Fig 13   Speed dribble 1: pushing the ball further out in front.

Fig 14   Speed dribble 2: push the ball out, because you will be dribbling in space.

Fig 15   Speed dribble 3: gathering the ball at the end of the bounce (*left*).

In order to protect the ball from a defender or to accelerate past your opponent you may well have to change hands while dribbling. Remember that when you change hands on the run you are not allowed to touch the ball with both hands at the same time. If you do, your dribble has ended, you come to a stop and must either pass the ball or shoot.

There are several ways you can change hands quickly and smoothly while dribbling the ball.

1. *Cross-over Dribble* Here you cross the ball over from one hand to the other in front of your body as you run. For

example, you bounce the ball across from your right hand to the left in front of you, enabling you to keep the ball away from a defender or to change the direction of your run.

It is important to keep the ball low as it passes in front of you – a quick, hard bounce means the ball is only out of your protection for as short a time as possible. Remember that the defender is always on the look-out for a steal.

When crossing the ball from the right hand to the left hand, have the right leg forward and the left leg back so that the ball crosses the gap between the legs.

This is the first technique to master in changing hands.

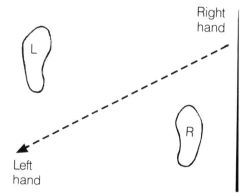

Fig 16 The between-the-legs dribble.

2. *Between-the-legs Dribble (Fig 16)* This looks 'flashier' and 'fancier' and is harder to master, but in fact is probably the safest way of changing hands. As its name suggests, it involves changing hands by passing the ball between your legs.

Passing from the right hand to the left, you place the left leg forward and the right leg to the rear, bouncing the ball between the legs and collecting it with the left hand.

You can see why this is a safe way of changing hands – the ball is protected during the change-over by the leading leg. *Remember* – keep your head up!

The next stage from this is to be able to bounce the ball between the legs while dribbling. Practise this at walking pace first, one bounce between the legs for every step.

3. *Behind-the-back Dribble (Fig 17)* The crowds love this, because like the between-the-legs dribble it looks 'flashy'. But, again, it is an excellent way of changing hands once you have mastered the difficult skills involved.

Changing the ball from right hand to left, you must wrap your fingers around the top, front part of the ball, pulling the ball back to the right of your backside. As it reaches that position, change the hand so that the fingers are now at the top, rear part of the ball and push it round to the left of the backside, where the ball is met after the bounce by the left hand, which continues the dribble.

The greatest fault with this dribble is that the dribbler may look down to see where the ball is, thus taking his eyes off his team-mates or defenders. But when you have this technique of the behind-

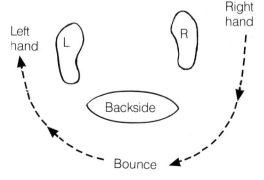

Fig 17 The behind-the-back dribble.

Fig 18   A between-the-legs dribble from former Bracknell player, Renaldo Lawrence (*opposite*).

the-back dribble in your basketball armoury, it is a great asset in throwing off defenders. Your aim eventually will be to execute the behind-the-back dribble at top speed.

4. Spin or Reverse Dribble (Fig 19) This method of changing hands involves turning full circle, 360 degrees, and at the same time changing hands. It is tough and will take a lot of practice, but it is worth it.

To change from a right-handed dribble to the left hand, place the left foot forward and pivot backwards on it. As you pivot, your left hand comes round and takes the ball which has been bounced by your right hand.

There is a danger in this move. As you spin, you face the wrong way for a

second, away from the basket you are attacking and away from your team-mates and the defenders. You must be quick.

TWO-BALL DRIBBLING
When you are proficient at these various dribbling techniques, here is a drill to make you sharper and faster.

Dribble two basketballs at the same time – one with each hand. At first do this standing still, then move slowly forward while you dribble, building up speed until eventually you can dribble with both hands at full speed. I know this is hard and it takes a lot of practice, but it is important to remember these points:

1. Keep your head up.
2. Look straight ahead.
3. Feel for the basketball.
4. Don't bounce the ball too high.
5. Bounce the balls alternately.

Got it? Excellent. Now do the double dribble going backwards and then to the side.

COACHING SESSION

Group Drills

DRIBBLING REACTION
Players form a line facing the coach, with a basketball each. On the whistle the players dribble the ball as quickly as possible towards the coach. When he raises his hand they stop immediately, holding the ball in both hands with the knees bent. On the whistle they set off again.

It is important that the stop signal comes from a raised hand, not from a whistle or a shout. This means that the players must keep their heads up while they are dribbling to watch for the signal.

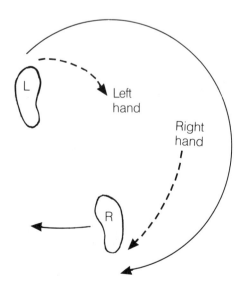

Fig 19   The spin, or reverse, dribble.

Repeat the drill dribbling with the left hand, then the right.

By raising his arm the coach can signal for the players to dribble to the left, the right, backwards or forwards, as well as telling them when they should stop the drill.

Remember – keep the head up or you will not know what to do.

DRIBBLE CHASE

In this drill there is one basketball for each pair of players. Using the full court the player without the ball runs anywhere across the floor, changing direction as often as he likes. His partner dribbles the ball and follows the leader, keeping as close as possible. The chase stops when the coach blows the whistle; the dribbler must then be within 3ft (1m) of the player without the ball.

This is a superb drill to incorporate the various techniques which have been practised up to this point. The dribbler must keep his head up at all times so that he can see the direction in which his partner is moving.

Changing hands in the dribble is also vital in this drill in order to protect the ball from collisions with the other players who are running the same exercise across the floor.

Fig 20 Ronnie Baker of England dribbling against a bigger player.

DRIBBLE TAG

Each player has a ball and is part of a group of six who will play in a confined area, such as the half-court. One player is the chaser and, dribbling the ball all the time, must try to catch the other players, who are also dribbling, and touch one of

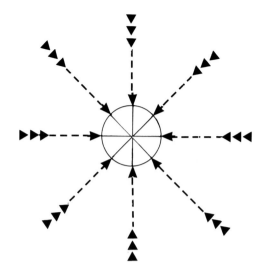

Fig 21   Practice for the 'heavy traffic' dribble.

them between the shoulder blades. Once touched, that player becomes the new chaser in the game of tag.

If a player loses control of the ball, he becomes the chaser.

This game requires close control, good vision by keeping the head up all the time to watch out for the chaser, and the ability to change speed and direction often and rapidly without losing control of the ball.

HEAVY TRAFFIC DRIBBLE *(Fig 21)*
The players divide into small, equal groups – eight groups of three, for example. The groups form around one of the court circles as in *Fig 21*.

The first player in each group has the basketball. On the whistle they dribble across to their groups on the opposite side of the circle.

Therefore, eight players, each with a ball, converge on the circle at the same time. This is what we call dribbling in 'heavy traffic'. Players must keep their heads up to watch out for the other players in order to protect the ball from collisions, change hands, and change speed and direction while keeping control of the ball.

When the dribblers reach the other side, they pass to the first person in the line and move to the back of the group.

DRIBBLE STEAL
Each player has a ball and plays in a designated area depending on numbers; ten players could use half of the court. They all dribble at the same time, the aim being to try to steal or knock away another player's ball while keeping control of their own.

You are out of the game if you move outside the designated area or if you touch the ball with both hands at the same time. Therefore, you are on a continuous dribble, and if the ball goes 'dead' on the floor you must get it started again by hitting it, *not* by picking it up.

As fewer players survive, the coach will restrict the playing area. When there are just three left in the game, they move into the centre circle on the court until the winner triumphs.

This is one of the best dribbling games, because while protecting your ball you must use your free hand to knock away someone else's ball. You must stay alert and keep your head up to watch for danger and opportunities.

RELAY DRIBBLES
Dribble along the floor using the right hand and then back with the left. As a variation, change hands at each marking on the court floor (i.e. foul line, half-way, foul line again, then the base line) by dribbling the ball between the legs, behind the back or with a spin dribble.

3
Pivoting

PROTECTING THE BALL

One of basketball's most important skills is being able to protect the ball from an opponent. You must be able to stop him stealing the ball from you. To do this, you have to learn the correct stance and the technique of pivoting.

Triple Threat Position *(Fig 22)*

When you receive the basketball you immediately pivot to face the basket you are attacking, and hold the ball in a position that gives your opponent the least possible chance of knocking it away from you.

Most beginners either hold the ball out in front or above their heads. Both positions are wrong, because the ball cannot be protected.

Here is the correct way. Hold the ball under the chin in both hands, using the finger pads and not the palms. Younger players will in fact be holding the ball on their upper chests. The elbows must be spread out for maximum protection. Finally, bend the knees as if you are about to sit on a chair. This is the triple threat position from which you can take the ball up to shoot, or pass or move into a dribble. You pose a triple threat to your opponent, and as long as you are protecting the ball you have the advantage, because he will not know what you are going to do.

Remember:

1. Extended elbows give protection.
2. Bent knees give a low position, balance and the ability to spring forward immediately. If your legs are straight you will

Fig 22   The triple threat position.

waste a valuable second bending them before you can move off.

3. Don't hold the ball too low. That may be good enough for a dribble, but not to shoot or to make a pass. You will therefore no longer be posing a triple threat to your opponent.

Technique

When you finish dribbling the ball, or before you start dribbling, you can pivot in order to protect the ball or to prepare to make a pass.

When pivoting, one foot remains on the floor – you must not move it. Imagine you have a six-inch nail through the ball of your foot into the court. You can lift your heel but can rotate only on the ball of your foot.

The pivot foot – the one that is nailed to the floor – is the foot that first touches the floor as you receive the basketball. This is usually the back foot. However, if you land with both feet hitting the floor at the same time as you receive the ball, you can choose which will be your pivot foot. Once you have decided, however, you cannot change your mind.

REVERSE PIVOT *(Fig 23)*
This is a backwards turn through 180 degrees pivoting on one foot.

FORWARD PIVOT *(Fig 24)*
This is a forwards turn through 180 degrees pivoting on one foot.

COACHING SESSION

Players should hold the ball in a protected triple threat position. The coach will instruct which foot is the pivot foot and whether to do a reverse or a forward pivot. Players then execute the moves on the whistle.

Remember – stay low, do not straighten when pivoting, stay balanced and keep your head up.

1 v 1 Pivoting

Allow one ball for each pair of players. The player with the ball adopts the triple threat position and can only pivot to keep the ball away from his partner, who must try to steal it.

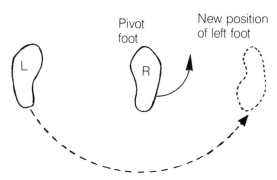

Fig 23   Reverse pivot: turning backwards by pivoting through 180 degrees.

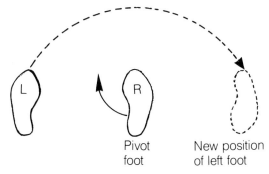

Fig 24   Forward pivot: turning forwards by pivoting through 180 degrees.

Fig 25 Chris Finch of the Sheffield Sharks protects the ball from the aggressive defensive play of Karl Brown of the London Leopards.

partners either side trying to take possession. This puts the pivoter under more pressure.

Remember – head up, elbows out, pivot quickly, keep your balance, lift the heel to pivot on the ball of the foot, and do not drag the foot across the floor.

Dribble and Pivot

Players dribble the ball and on the whistle make a balanced jump stop, hitting the floor with both feet at the same time. The coach shouts which foot to pivot on, and whether to make a forward or reverse pivot. *Remember* – take up a triple threat position when you stop.

Instead of shouting or using the whistle the coach can raise a hand to signal the stop, ensuring that the players have their heads up at all times.

The player with the ball must keep his head up to watch his partner. Make a mark on the floor for the pivot foot, to ensure that it does not drag along. Change over after a set time.

1 v 2 Pivoting

Players divide into groups of three, the pivoter holding the ball and the two

Jump Stop Practice

Players run all over the court and on the whistle make an immediate jump stop, placing both feet on the floor at the same time without overbalancing.

4
Passing

Young players learning basketball are happy enough to practise dribbling and shooting at every opportunity, but they are not so ready to practise passing on their own. Not enough emphasis is placed on the importance of passing to the game of basketball. Passing has become a 'lost art', but don't let it become that for you.

Remember, basketball is a team game played with up to ten players on the floor at the same time. That is a very small space for all those players, so your passing will have to be good or the ball will be lost or stolen

If you work hard and become an excellent passer you will always find a team to play for, because your ability will prove you are an unselfish team player, the sort that every basketball club wants to have.

TYPES OF PASS

Chest Pass *(Figs 26 to 30)*

This is probably the most common pass in basketball and is used when no defender is in the way. The ball moves from the passer's chest to where the receiver is signalling, either to his hand or where he is pointing. If the receiver does not signal, then the ball should be passed to his chest.

Hold the ball between your finger pads; your palms do not touch the ball.

The fingertips should be each side of the ball and you should try to make your thumbs meet behind the ball. The ball is held to your chest with the elbows extended. The pass is started as you step forward, thus moving your body in the direction of the pass to give power and balance while releasing the ball.

Fig 26   Chest pass 1: the fingertips are on the ball with the thumbs meeting behind; hold the ball to the chest with the elbows extended.

33

Fig 27   Move the body in the direction of the pass, extending the arms away from the chest.

Fig 28   Fingers point to the receiver, thumbs point down; snap the wrists.

Fig 29   The receiver signals with the hand furthest away from the defender.

As you step forward, extend the arms away from your chest; when they are straight, snap the wrists out simultaneously. Your fingers should end up pointing to the receiver with the thumbs pointing down at the floor. The snap of the wrists is important as it makes the pass crisp and firm.

The chest pass should travel in a straight line to the receiver, who signals to receive it with the hand furthest away from the defender. If he is unguarded, then he signals to receive it with the hand outstretched in the direction he is moving. The receiver takes a step forward to meet the ball and immediately gathers it into the protected position against the chest, below the chin.

Bounce Pass *(Figs 31 & 32)*

This is a useful pass – but be careful! The bounce pass can be dangerous so be

Fig 30   The chest pass should travel in a straight line.

Fig 31   For the bounce pass, move the ball to the hip in
both hands, then push away with one hand.

Fig 32   The ball bounces once past your opponent.

sure of when it can be used, namely when you need to get the ball past an opponent to the receiver.

The bounce can be made with one or two hands, but it is usually made with one. Hold the ball in two hands and step in the direction of the pass, let's say to the right. Move the ball to your right hip, still held in both hands, then push it away with the right hand to bounce once on the floor, past your opponent and to the receiver.

Here are the dangers: because the ball hits the floor the pass is slower and therefore easier to intercept; and the ball may not bounce high enough to be caught comfortably. So, to counteract these dangers, make the bounce quickly – and hard.

Overhead Pass *(Figs 33 to 35)*

This is also executed to get the ball past a defender and, of course, it is made over the head.

Hold the ball between the finger pads in the same way as for the chest pass, but directly over the head.

Again, step in the direction of the pass, move your arms slightly forward and snap the wrists as you release the ball. The fingers point at the receiver, with the thumbs pointing down at the floor.

The ball should travel in a straight line, to the receiver's signal or his chest area, which is the easiest place to catch the ball.

This is an important and frequent pass, particularly when a rebounder has taken possession and makes an 'outlet' pass to

Fig 33   The overhead pass: hold the ball between the fingertips, directly over the head.

Fig 34   Move your arms slightly forward and step in the direction of the pass.

Fig 35 Snap the wrists on release. The fingers should point at the receiver, with the thumbs closest to the floor.

a team-mate, or when a pass is made to a team-mate standing under your opponent's basket.

Javelin or Baseball Pass

This pass has a one-handed action and is used in certain situations to throw the ball a long distance up the court.

In a right-handed pass, place the left leg forward in a balanced stance. Lift the ball with two hands, then take it behind the head at arm's length with the right hand at shoulder height. Then throw the ball like a javelin or a baseball – the elbows bend first, the arm comes through and the wrist snaps as the ball is released, the fingers pointing in the direction of the pass.

As with the bounce pass, there are dangers and weaknesses. Firstly, when the ball is being held behind the head it is unprotected and can easily be knocked away. When you prepare to make the javelin pass, make sure that no defenders are near.

Secondly, because it is a one-handed pass you are committed to releasing the ball once you have started moving your arm forward. If a defender steps in front of your receiver as you are about to release the ball, he will intercept the pass.

So, whenever possible, try to make passes with two hands.

The javelin pass tends to be less accurate, particularly as it is used over long distances – for example, when you want to fling the ball to a team-mate who is at the other end of the court. Because of this, use the pass only to an unmarked team-mate when there is no chance of interception.

Finally, although it is a one-handed pass and you may be left- or right-handed, the javelin pass must be practised with both hands.

INDIVIDUAL PRACTICE

As passing needs two players it is not an easy technique to practise on your own. This is why young players often do not pass well, whereas they can practise dribbling and shooting on their own.

A wall is your best partner if you have to practise passing completely on your own. Vary the distance you stand away from the wall and practise all of the passes mentioned in the chapter so far. As you improve, use chalk marks to make targets on the wall.

Remember, the ball must travel in a straight line. Follow the correct technique to make crisp and sharp passes. Do not make lob or looping passes, as during the game they would take too long to reach your team-mate.

Now you are ready to really test yourself. Draw a series of squares or circles on the wall at different heights (Fig 36). Your family or friends may not want to pass the ball with you, but they can help in this drill. Ask them to shout numbers in random sequence. Each shouted number will represent a different square or circle on the wall and a particular type of pass. At the shout 'one' you must hit that number with the specified pass, in this case a left-handed bounce pass. Here is a list you can use:

1. Left-handed bounce pass.
2. Left-handed baseball pass.
3. Overhead pass.
4. Chest pass or two-handed bounce pass.
5. Right-handed baseball pass.
6. Right-handed bounce pass.

See how many marks you can hit correctly in succession or in a time limit – thirty seconds or a minute, perhaps.

COACHING SESSION

Group Practices

TWO-MAN PASSES
Each pair of players, roughly matching in age and size, shares a basketball.

One player makes a chest pass to his partner, remembering the correct technique of step and pass, and step to receive pass. The receiver has his hands outstretched to take the ball, which should travel in a straight line from his partner's chest to his chest.

The pairs then make a bounce pass, again ensuring the correct technique in every stage of the move.

Then the pairs move further apart, to between 15ft and 20ft (4.5m and 6m) to

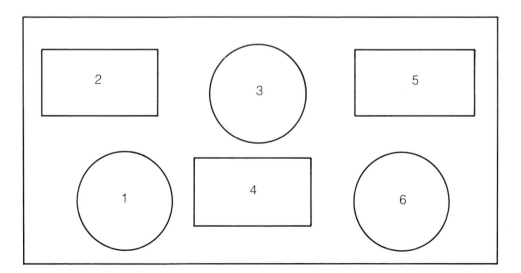

Fig 36   Practising against a wall; each number represents a particular type of pass.

Fig 37   Steve Nelson of Worthing looking to make an overhead pass over the shorter Alton Byrd (*opposite*).

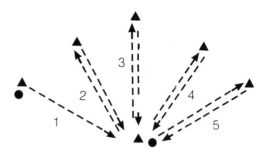

Fig 38   Pepper-pot passing.

make an overhead pass. This is *not* a soccer throw-in. In a basketball overhead pass the ball is held above the head, *not* behind it.

Finally, the pairs move further apart from each other to make the baseball or javelin pass.

TWO-MAN ALTERNATE PASSING

Players divide into pairs with one ball each and stand about 10ft (3m) apart. One player makes a chest pass to his partner, who simultaneously makes a bounce pass.

This is a great drill to teach how to handle pressure passing, because the instant you have released the ball you must be ready to receive a pass from your partner. Use this practice once you have mastered the technique for each pass, all of which can be used in this pressure situation. Beginners should not attempt this drill, because if they have not mastered passing techniques they will simply throw the ball at each other in any fashion.

PEPPER-POT PASSING *(Fig 38)*

Players divide into groups of six with two balls for each group; five of the players form a shallow semicircle with the sixth man facing them.

The drill begins with one ball at the end of the semicircle and the other with the player facing the other five. The player on the end of the arc passes the ball to the player facing the arc, who simultaneously passes his ball to the second player in the semicircle. The second player passes the ball back to the player facing the arc, who

simultaneously passes his ball to the third player in the semicircle, and so on.

LONG (OR FULL) COURT PASSING

Each pair of players shares one ball and begins by facing the backboard at one end of the court. As one player throws the ball against the backboard his partner turns and sprints away down the court.

The first player catches the ball, pivots, then throws a baseball, or javelin, pass to his partner, who by now should be almost at the other end of the court. He catches the ball and scores. The first player, immediately after releasing the pass, sprints down the floor to gather the rebound from his partner's shot.

This is a good drill for making a pass to a moving team-mate. Ensure correct technique is used. The running partner must signal for the ball with an outstretched hand, and the first player should aim just in front of the signal so that the second player can run on to the pass and score.

To add competition, the coach can stand on the half-way line to obstruct the pass. The passer must now aim the ball over this 'defender'. Obviously, this drill is for older players who have the strength to throw the ball the whole length of the court.

41

THREE-MAN PASSING ON THE MOVE

Each group of three players shares one ball, and they set up under the basket with one player in the middle and the others at either side.

The player in the middle makes a chest pass to the receiver's signal on one side, takes the return pass and then passes to the player on the other side. The trio of players moves down the court.

Ensure you follow the correct technique in making the pass, in receiving the pass by signalling with outstretched hand, and that you do not run with the ball.

As soon as the first group reaches the half-way line, the next group moves off. All groups wait at the other end until every trio has finished.

THREE-MAN WEAVE *(Fig 39)*

This is based on the three-man passing move, except that the player who passes the ball runs around behind the receiver. At first it is a hard drill because it involves a lot of passing and needs great accuracy. But when the three-man weave has been mastered, it definitely helps a player's ability to watch and pass at the same time.

The players should start by weaving slowly, before speeding up as they become used to the movement.

PIG IN THE MIDDLE

This drill uses a defender, putting more pressure on the passers. A group of three players shares one ball, with the two outside players each about 15ft (5m) from the player in the middle. One outside player has the ball.

1. The middle player moves to within 2ft (60cm) of the outside player (who has the ball).

2. The player with the ball must pass to his partner without the man in the middle getting a touch. If the ball is intercepted with a touch, the passer moves into the middle and the 'defender' moves to the outside.

3. Passers are not allowed to lob the ball over the man in the middle, but must make a direct pass.

4. The passer must follow the correct technique by taking a step towards the defender (using the pivot), by protecting the ball, and by making a crisp, level pass.

5. Some beginners turn away from a defender to protect the ball. They must face the defender, with the ball protected in the triple threat position, and pass the ball correctly and confidently.

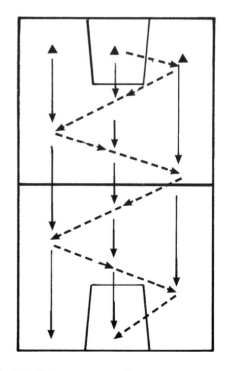

Fig 39   Three-man passing weave.

6. As players improve they should have a time limit of, say, three seconds before they must pass the ball. If the passer fails to beat the time limit he must move into the middle.

7. The receiver is restricted to making one step to the left or the right to collect the pass. If the pass is so wide that he cannot catch the ball after taking a step, then the passer must move into the middle.

PASSING LANES

At this point I shall break off to talk briefly about the passing lanes. The passing lanes are:

1. Over the top of the head.
2. Either side of the defender's head.
3. Either side of the defender's feet.
4. Under the defender's arms. But be warned – this is very difficult; you must be an inch-perfect passer before

Fig 40 England captain Peter Scantlebury reaching to receive a pass whilst playing for his club team, Thames Valley Tigers, against Bologna of Italy.

43

attempting to pass the ball through this gap.

These passing lanes are the hardest places for a defender to reach quickly with his hands. It is not enough simply to aim the ball at one of the passing lanes and hope for the best. You must 'fake' the defender before passing through one of the passing lanes.

A 'fake' is when you move to pass the ball but hold on to it. If you do it properly the defender will be committed to cutting off a pass which will never take place.

If you fake to pass the ball over the defender's head he will automatically raise his hands. That is when the passer steps past the defender's foot and makes a bounce pass to a team-mate.

If you fake to pass the ball close to the defender's foot, he will reach down with his hands. That is when you send the pass whistling by his ear. But you have to be quick as well. If the defender is not fooled into dropping his hands to cut off the fake, then you make the original pass close to his feet.

BULL IN A CIRCLE

Five or six players form a circle around a player. A player in the circle has the ball and must pass to another player over or around the man in the middle. If the 'bull' in the middle of the ring touches the ball then he swaps places with the passer.

This drill can be expanded; for example, with ten players, move three into the middle. The passes must be direct – no lobs! As always, follow the correct technique. Take a step to pass the ball and fake the defender by looking one way and then passing in another direction.

This is excellent practice for game situations. It is a very competitive drill – but very enjoyable, particularly if the man in the middle works hard to try to cut off the passes, and if his opponents make clean, crisp passes. Lob passes are not allowed, as in a real game they are the most likely to be intercepted.

KEEP IT!

This is a super practice, combining all of the passes covered in this chapter, as well as pivoting and protecting the ball. This drill is used by many coaches and can also be used as a warm-up.

The players divide into two teams, wearing either different coloured shirts or bands. For five-a-side use half the court, or the whole court for ten-a-side. The coach throws the ball into the air and whichever team gets possession must make ten consecutive passes without the other team intercepting or stealing the ball. If possession is lost, then the new team must make ten passes.

No dribbling is allowed so all of the different aspects of passing must be used – protecting the ball, making crisp and firm passes, pivoting and moving in order to get into position for a better pass.

All the different passes are used: chest pass – short passes; bounce pass – to get the ball past an opponent; baseball pass – reaching a team-mate down the court.

Once the teams become fast and sure, introduce another rule. The ball must not be returned to the player who has just passed it to you. This means that players must work ever harder to get free and make good, safe passes. With a beginners' group, the numbers of consecutive passes can be reduced to five or seven.

5
Shooting

Given a basketball, most people will set off on a dribble straight away, followed by a shot at the basket. Shooting is undoubtedly the most popular part of basketball. Sadly, the lack of outside basketball courts in Britain means it is not always easy to find a basket to shoot at.

The other skills we have mentioned so far – passing, dribbling and pivoting – can all be practised away from the court and without a basketball ring. So, when you have a basket to shoot at, do not waste time. It is vital that you practise shooting correctly. There are several different kinds of shot and we begin dealing with them here.

LAY-UP SHOT

The lay-up is a moving shot made close to the basket. When you shoot from the right-hand side of the basket, you shoot with the right hand. You jump from the left leg for a right-handed shot and have your right knee raised.

When dribbling on the move you can take two steps after picking the ball up. Therefore, for a right-handed lay-up your two steps will be right foot, left foot, jumping off the left foot and raising the right knee, then shooting the ball with the right hand softly against the backboard so that it is deflected down into the net. Most backboards have a small square marked

Fig 41   Adrian Jones of the London Leopards scoring against Worthing.

above the ring; you should aim for the top right-hand corner of this square.

When you dribble in from the left-hand side, the technique for the right-handed shot is simply reversed.

45

Learning the Lay-up

1. Stand one pace away, feet together, to the right of the basket. Take the ball up in both hands with the right hand underneath it. As you begin the shot, lift the right knee, straighten the right arm and flick the wrist so that the ball is propelled softly against the top right-hand corner of the small square.
2. Take a further step back, feet together, then step forward and jump off the left leg, lift the right knee and shoot with the right hand.
3. Take another step back. Step forward with the right leg, then the left and jump from the left leg, lift the right knee and shoot with the right hand.
4. Start with the left foot forward and bounce the ball beside the right leg with the right hand. As you bounce the ball lift the right leg, catch the ball, place the right leg down, then the left and jump from the left, lifting the right knee and shooting with the right hand.

Learners can be helped by chalk marks drawn on the floor.

As players become proficient they can start further away from the basket, dribble the ball in with the right hand, pick up the ball, step with the right leg, then the

Fig 42   Stephane Ostrowski of France uses the backboard to protect his lay-up against Spain.

Fig 43   Stephen Hansell of the Birmingham Bullets demonstrates great athletic ability as he soars to shoot at the basket.

left, jump from the left, lift the right knee and then shoot with the right hand.

While shooting the lay-up you use your other arm and your body to protect the ball. If a defender tries to stop your shot he will probably hit part of your body, or your arm, and therefore commit a foul.

Always use the backboard when making the shot as it will compensate for slight inaccuracy. You can shoot the ball high on the square or low, but it will still drop into the basket. You have to be much more accurate to score directly into the basket.

Practices

LAY-UP LINES *(Fig 44)*

Players form two lines to the left and right of the basket, just inside the half-way line. The right-hand line has two basketballs.

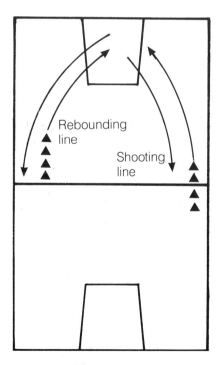

Rebounding line

Shooting line

Fig 44   Lay-up lines.

The first player from the right dribbles in, shoots a right-hand lay-up and continues on to the back of the left-hand line, while the player from the front of the left-hand line runs in to collect the rebound. He passes the ball to the next player at the front of the right-hand line, while he himself runs to the back of that line. From then on this drill just rolls along. The shooter from the right-hand line runs to the back of the left-hand line, to become a rebounder next time around, while the rebounder from the left-hand line moves to the back of the right-hand line to become a shooter.

Besides the lay-up, this exercise also practises rebounding, dribbling and passing. Make sure the players jump to take the rebound, even if the ball drops through the basket. When every player has made several right-hand lay-ups, switch lines so that the shooters come in from the left for a left-hand shot.

QUICK-FIRE LAY-UPS *(Fig 45)*

In this drill each group of four players has two balls, and each group stands at a basket. One player stands at the foul line, two stand about 12ft (3.5m) out to the side of the key area and the fourth stands under a basket as a rebounder.

Player 1 runs to the basket, receives a pass from Player 2 and shoots a right-hand lay-up before running back to his starting position. Player 4 rebounds the ball and passes it back to Player 2.

As soon as Player 1 returns to the start, he turns and runs back to the basket, takes a pass from Player 3 and shoots a left-hand lay-up before returning again. Player 4 rebounds the ball and passes to Player 3.

As soon as Player 1 reaches the start again he turns to go for another right-hand lay-up, repeating the first drill.

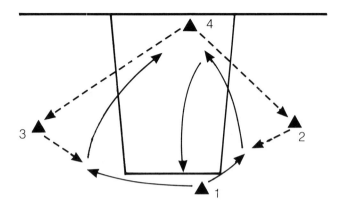

Fig 45   Quick-fire lay-ups.

This is a continuous drill to be run to either a time limit (baskets scored in one minute, for example) or how many attempts it takes to score ten baskets. It involves left- and right-hand lay-ups as well as passing and rebounding.

The shooter must signal for the pass as he runs to the basket, by stretching out the arm nearest to the basket – left hand for a right lay-up and vice versa.

Concentrate on the correct technique and on using the backboard by releasing the ball high and soft onto the target square.

1 ON 1 LAY-UP PRACTICE *(Fig 46)*
In this exercise each pair of players has one ball. The player with the ball starts on the right-hand side of the court between 6ft and 10ft (1.8m and 3m) in front of his part-

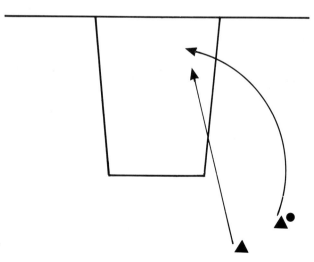

Fig 46   1 on 1 lay-up practice.

ner, depending on the ability of the players. On the whistle the first player runs to attempt a right-hand lay-up and his partner follows in an attempt to try to stop the shot.

This is a game situation practice so all of the correct techniques must be used. Dribble with the head up and run in a straight line. A curved run takes longer and therefore gives the defender more time to cut off the attack.

As the players improve, the starting distance between them will be cut, but the shooter must protect the ball all the time he is dribbling and making the lay-up.

If the defender can get in front, the attacker will be forced to stop and attempt a set shot or jump shot.

SET AND JUMP SHOTS

In order to execute a lay-up in a basketball match you need space – either space between defenders or a clear run at the basket to dribble, take two steps and shoot. But more experienced and better organized teams will not allow you that space. There must be another way of scoring, and the most common scoring shot in basket is the *set shot* or *jump shot*.

Set Shot Technique

1. The feet point in the direction of the shot, which is aimed either directly at the basket or at the square drawn on the backboard if the shot is to be 'banked' off the backboard into the ring. If the shot is being attempted from

Fig 47 Use of the left hand and total concentration by Alfonso Reyes of Spain as he scores against Greece.

Fig 48　Jim Bilba of France drives between two Croatian defenders to score.

the side, or wing, it is best to use the backboard. The feet should be shoulder-width apart in a relaxed, balanced stance.

2. The knees should be slightly bent or flexed, as they will give the power to the shot.

3. The shoulders should be squarely facing the basket. Do not turn them to shoot.

4. The ball rests on the finger pads of the shooting hand, never on the palm. To check, place a finger from the other hand between the ball and the palm of the shooting hand. If you cannot get through the gap, the ball is on the palm.

5. The wrist of the shooting hand is bent back to form a platform for the ball. The elbow is directly under the ball, directed at the basket. The upper arm is level with the shoulder and at a right angle to the lower arm.

6. The non-shooting hand is placed to the side of the ball as a support.

7. In preparing to shoot, the ball is held in both hands, slightly above and in front of the head. The eyes are focused on the top corner of the nearest edge of the black square drawn on the backboard. If the shot is aimed directly at the basket, concentrate on the rear third of the ring.

8. To start the shot, straighten the legs and the arms, and as the shooting arm reaches full stretch the supporting arm snaps forward so that the fingers end up pointing at the basket.

9. The arm should finish at an angle of forty-five degrees as this gives the best flight path to the ball. Remember, the ring is 10ft (3m) above the ground so you must send the ball in an arc higher than 10ft (3m) for it to drop down through the basket.

10. The snap of the wrist is essential as it gives the ball backspin. When the ball hits the backboard the backspin deadens the force of the shot and it will drop softly through the hoop. Basketball players talk about 'touch' and 'feel' when they refer to the backspin they put on the ball.

JUMP SHOT *(Figs 49 to 52)*
The difference between a set shot and a jump shot is obvious. The jump shot is launched at the top of a jump, but using the same technique as for the set shot.

It is important that you jump vertically and land in the same place. Do not drift forward when making a jump shot.

As players become older and stronger they will attempt jump shots rather than set shots. The jump shot is better, for one reason because it is launched from higher up and is therefore harder to stop. The set shot is launched from a standing position, which makes it easier to block.

Beginners should not attempt jump shots until they have mastered the technique of performing set shots. If beginners try the jump shot before they are strong enough, they get into bad habits and will throw the ball as in a soccer throw or launch shots from a chest pass position.

Individual Practices

1. *Ten in a Row* Stand one step away at forty-five degrees to the backboard and basket, adopt the correct stance and shoot either a set or a jump shot. Rebound the shot and move away to shoot again, using the backboard if you are at the side. Score ten in a row, then take a further step away from the basket and repeat the procedure.

Score another ten then move another pace away. By now you should be at the edge of the key. Every time you make ten

51

Fig 49   The jump shot: the feet point in the direction of the shot with the shoulders squarely facing the basket. The knees should be slightly flexed to give power to the shot.

Fig 50   Note the elbow of the shooting arm is directly under the ball, with the upper arm level with the shoulder and at a right angle to the lower arm.

Fig 51   The jump shot is launched at the top of the jump.

Fig 52   When taking a jump shot it is important to jump vertically and land in the same place.

Fig 53   Excellent follow-through demonstrated by a Russian player in the European Championship game against Ukraine.

in a row move further away. If you fail to hit ten shots, go back to zero and stay where you are.

A common fault with young players when practising shooting is that they move too far away before they are ready. With this drill you do not move away until your technique is good enough for you to hit the target. The further you are from the target, the more you use your legs. That is where the strength and lift for the shot come from. The arm action remains the same whatever the shooting distance.

There is no short cut to becoming a great shooter. It takes hours of practice, always using the correct technique. Without the technique your shot will break down and you will be unable to score even from close range, let alone mid- or long distance. The more you practise the easier and more natural the technique will become. You will be comfortable with your shot. Good shooters know their best shooting distance – and stick to it.

2. *Toss and Shoot* Stand with the ball within your shooting range then lob it softly in the direction of the basket. After one bounce catch the ball, pivot to face the basket, then shoot (either a set or jump shot, depending on age and strength), run to get the rebound then repeat the drill.

This practice represents receiving a pass before shooting. Make sure you are balanced and facing the basket when you shoot. Carefully follow the technique and use the backboard when shooting from the wing.

3. *Around the World* (*Fig 54*) Start at the edge of the key by the first mark closest to the basket. Shoot, and if you score move to the next mark out. See how many shots it takes you to move to all the

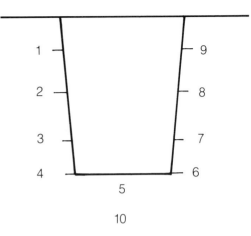

Fig 54   Around the world.

marks round the key. Play against a friend and race to see who is the first to finish. Shots can also be tried from the very top of the key.

This is a good practice and competitive fun as the shots will be in the range of all young players.

4. *Dribble Shoot* The player with the ball dribbles to the left or right of the basket, taking one or two bounces, then stops and shoots using all the correct techniques. He takes his rebound and repeats the procedure. Take just one or two bounces, dribble the ball quickly, keep your head up and look at the basket, and keep the ball low. Stop and make sure of your balance before shooting. When shooting the jump shot, ensure you jump and land at the same spot. See how many shots it takes to score ten baskets.

Group Practices

1. *21 Up* (*Fig 55*) Players group into twos, threes or even fours, sharing one ball to each group. Up to three groups stand at

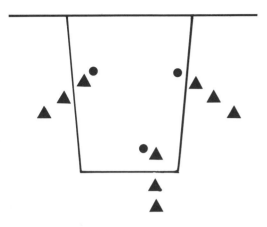

Fig 55   21 up.

one basket and they shoot within their range.

On the whistle, the first person in the group shoots and runs to get the rebound. If the ball goes in, the group scores two points. If the ball misses but the player can take the rebound before the ball hits the floor and then scores, the team gets one point. If the player scores with the first shot, catches the ball before it hits the floor and scores again, the total is three points. Two shots per go is the maximum. If the player misses with the first jump shot and the ball hits the floor, no points are scored. The player with the ball turns back to the group, passes the ball to the player at the front and moves to the back of the line.

The first team to reach twenty-one points wins. This drill involves shooting, rebounding and passing under the pressure of competition. If a shot is knocked away from the basket by the other team's ball . . .hard luck!

2. *Rotation Shooting* (*Fig 56*) The organization of this drill depends on how many baskets are available at the gym. For example, if there are four baskets, have six players at a basket divided into two teams of three. Each team has one ball.

On the whistle, the first person shoots to score one basket, then, whether he scores or not, rebounds and passes to the next person in the team and runs to the back of the team. The first team to score four baskets runs to the centre circle to win.

The teams start in the position shown in *Fig 56*. On the second whistle they rotate one position clockwise round the court to face a new team: 2 v 3, 4 v 5, 6 v 7, 8 v 1. On the whistle the shooting starts again. The first team to win three shoot-outs are the champions.

Concentrate on technique and shooting within a comfortable distance, shown by chalk marks on the floor. Shooting,

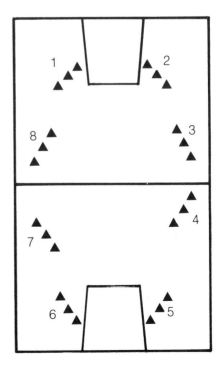

Fig 56   Rotation shooting.

55

passing, rebounding and running are all part of this drill, plus the excitement of competition.

3. *'Gotcha'* This is a highly competitive shooting game for players with sound technique and a good shooting range. If there are ten players keep them in one group, but split twenty players into two groups. Each group has two balls and lines up in file starting at the foul line. The first two players have a ball each.

On the whistle the first player shoots, rebounding if he misses to shoot again. If the ball bounces a long way from the basket the player can dribble in, using the correct technique, to shoot again.

The player tries to score as quickly as possible because as soon as he launches his first shot the second player can shoot from the same distance. If the second player in the pair scores first, then the first player is out – 'Gotcha'.

If Player 1 scores first, he quickly passes to the third player in line, who tries to eliminate the second player. So the drill goes on, with players moving to the back of the line after scoring. Eventually there will be just two players left in a 'play-off', with the survivor the champion.

Remember, a player is 'got' only if the player behind scores first.

This is one of the best shooting games I have played. It uses shooting, rebounding, scoring and passing, all under pressure; but the players must follow the correct technique.

4. *H-O-R-S-E* There is lots of fun and enjoyment to be had from this shooting game for two or more players away from formal training sessions.

The first player shoots from anywhere he wishes. If he scores then the next player must copy his shot from the same spot on the floor. If he also scores, the next player copies and so on. If a player misses the copied shot he gets the letter 'H'. Then the next player in the line makes a fresh shot from a different spot and the other players, in turn, must try to copy him.

Any kind of shot can be used – jump shot, lay-up or set shot. As soon as a player has missed enough shots that his letters spell 'horse', then he is out of the game. Play until there is a winner. Use the letters for P-I-G for a shorter game, played to exactly the same rules.

FREE THROW OR FOUL SHOT
(Figs 57 to 63)

This is the shot that every player *must* be able to score successfully.

There will be times in a match – such as when a player is fouled during the act of shooting – when free throws are awarded. This is like a penalty in soccer. You always take this shot from the free-throw line, which is 15ft (4.6m) away from the basket. Once the match official hands you the ball you have five seconds to make the shot. No one is allowed to stop you. The only limits are the time allowed and that the feet must not cross the foul line.

This situation is always the same, whatever the match. Each free shot you score is worth one point, instead of two points for a normal 'field' basket.

The technique is almost the same as for a set shot. Face the basket with the feet behind the foul line, shoulder-width apart, and with the knees bent. Develop your own routine for attempting the free throw and always stick to it.

Bounce the ball a couple of times to gain composure, look at the basket and

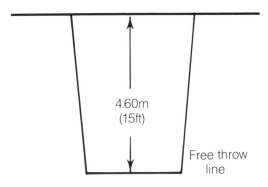

4.60m
(15ft)

Free throw
line

Fig 57   The free throw.

bend the knees. As you straighten the knees, straighten the shooting arm and flick the wrist as you shoot the ball. Aim for the rear third of the ring.

If your shot repeatedly hits the front of the ring, bend the legs a little more and shoot the ball in a higher arc so that it will drop down through the ring. If the ball keeps hitting the back of the ring, make less use of your legs and do not flick the ball away so hard.

Fig 58   England International Karl Brown prepares to release the ball on his free throw.

57

Fig 59   The free throw: face the basket, with the feet shoulder-width apart behind the foul line.

Fig 60   Look at the basket, bend the knees.

Fig 61   As you straighten the knees, straighten the shooting arm and flick the wrist as you shoot the ball.

Fig 62   Concentrate on the follow-through and getting the right arc on the shot.

Fig 63 Composure and concentration on the free-throw line by Vlade Divac of Yugoslavia and the Los Angeles Lakers.

The secret of being a good free-throw shooter – and this applies to all the shots in basketball – is *practice*. Always practise the free throws when you have the chance. Aim for at least ten a day and record how many you score out of each set of ten. If you have a partner, compete against him.

Get into a free-throw routine and keep to it! Whenever I shoot a free throw I:

1. Line up my right foot with the centre of the basket and my left foot to the side.
2. Bounce the ball three times.
3. Bring the ball up to the shooting position, take a deep breath and shoot,

concentrating on the follow-through and getting the right arc on the shot.

You should *never* miss a free throw. You must practise, practise, practise.

CLOSE TO THE BASKET SHOTS

So far we have looked at the lay-up shot and the set or jump shot, and have described the correct technique and practice drills. In basketball games you will often be near to the basket but closely defended. Therefore it is essential to be able to shoot the ball well when under pressure.

There are three kinds of shots close to the basket: the power move, the hook shot and the dunk shot.

Power Move

A power move is made close to the basket under pressure from defenders. Make sure that you are balanced, and that your shoulders and feet are parallel to the baseline.

It is important that once you begin the power move you jump strongly towards the basket and shoot softly towards the backboard. If you are at the right-hand side of the basket you should shoot with your right hand (hand furthest away from the defender), or with the left hand from the left side of the basket.

If you are making a power move against a bigger person you should fake first to get the defender off balance, then make your power move.

With a power move the attacking player should either score or draw the foul each time.

Be ready for contact with defenders but still get your shot away.

PRACTICES

1. *Lay-up Lines* In this drill the player dribbles as in the lay-up practice, but instead makes the power move. Stop with a jump, take a balanced position and power up to score the basket.

Remember to practise the power moves from both the right and the left sides of the basket.

2. *1 v 1 Power Move* Here we have one attacker and one defender. The attacker dribbles the ball to the power move position and then powers up to take his shot. The defender puts some pressure on the attacker; initially he just exerts token pressure but gradually increases his activity until it is a realistic game situation. If the attacker misses his shot then he should get the rebound and power it up into the basket. Practise the drill from either side.

3. *Mass Power Move Game* Four players stand at one basket and when the ball is thrown up at the basket all four go for the rebound. Whoever takes the rebound tries to score with a power move. The ball is always in play, so whoever takes the ball after the basket shoots immediately with a power move. This is, therefore, a continuous practice in which the person with the ball is shooting under pressure against the other three defending players.

The drill is played until one player has scored three baskets to win the game. Remember to use the left hand from the left side of the basket and fake the defender to make him jump out of position.

Hook Shot *(Figs 64 & 65)*

The hook shot is again used when the attacker is close to the basket but not as close as for the power move. The shot is started initially from the edge of the key and is a modification of a lay-up as the shooter jumps off one leg.

This shot is usually taken by post players (i.e. the taller members of the team), who receive the ball with their backs to the basket. Therefore, if the attacker receives the ball on the left side of the key with his back to the basket, he pivots on his right foot and steps with his left foot across the key parallel to the basket. The shooter jumps off his left leg, lifts his right knee (just as in a lay-up) and takes the ball up in two hands. As he jumps, the ball is taken up in the right hand with the arm fully extended, the wrist flicking through so that the ball spins and the shot is soft when it hits the ring.

Practise the hook shot with both the right and the left hands.

PRACTICES

1. *Continuous Hook Shots* A player stands with his back to the basket two steps away from the backboard. The player steps with the left foot and shoots a right-hand hook shot. As the ball goes through the basket he takes the rebound, then steps with the right foot the other way to shoot a left-hand hook shot. The rebound is taken again, followed by a right-hand hook. Therefore, the player shoots continuous right- and left-hand shots.

See how many shots you can make out of ten or how many you can score in thirty seconds.

2. *1 v 1 Hook Shot* There are two players – one attacker and one defender. The attacking player starts with the ball, fakes to go right, then with the left foot steps to shoot a right-hand hook shot. Initially, the

Fig 64 The hook shot: looking at the basket and preparing to shoot.

Fig 65 Jump off the right leg, with right knee lifted and right arm fully extended, and the wrist snapping through.

defence is very passive, then gradually becomes more intense.

If the defender stands to the attacker's left to stop him taking a right-hand hook shot, then the attacker should pivot the other way and dribble the ball to the power move position and shoot a power move. Thus the attacking player can combine both the hook shot and the power move.

Remember to practise with both the right and the left hands.

Dunk Shot

The dunk shot is the most impressive, spectacular and entertaining in basketball. In this shot the player jumps so that his arms are above the level of the ring and throws the ball down through the basket.

This can be done in a variety of ways: a player can dunk with one hand, or both hands, forwards or backwards, and with a running jump or from a standing jump.

Although a basket with a dunk shot is still only worth two points it can really stimulate the attacking team and demoralize the defence. However, it is important to remember that a missed dunk can have exactly the opposite effect: it can stimulate the defending team and demoralize the offensive team, particularly if the score is close at the time of the miss.

In order to dunk the ball you need to have good timing and obviously have to

61

Fig 66   The 7ft 2in (2.2m) tall Arvidas Sabonis dunks in the European Championship final against Yugoslavia.

be able to jump so that your hand is over the height of the ring (10ft/3m).

PRACTICES
To be able to dunk you must be able to jump, and therefore you must build up your jumping ability. Start by trying to touch the net with a running jump, then touch the backboard, then work up the net until you can touch the ring. Once you can touch the ring try to dunk a table-tennis ball or a golf ball, then a volleyball or football, and eventually a basketball.

Take a normal lay-up, but instead of shooting the ball off the backboard, jump with the ball above the ring and push it down through the basket.

Once you can dunk with one hand, try with two. A two-handed dunk is safer than the one-handed as there is less chance of the basketball slipping out of your hands.

Remember that dunking is very entertaining and impressive but it is not the be-all and end-all of being a basketball player. You might be an exceptional dunker, but if you can't dribble, shoot, pass or defend well you will never become a good basketball player.

6
Individual Defence

Young players will not naturally practise defending on their own. Naturally, they want to attack and will happily run through the various drills for dribbling, shooting and passing. Basketball, however, is one of the few sports where defending actually adds to the excitement of the game. Because of the time limits imposed during a game, the teams are under pressure to attack quickly. They are allowed just ten seconds to get the ball over the half-way line and a total of thirty seconds to attempt a shot at the other team's basket.

There are few tactics more exciting in basketball than a full court press, where the defending team goes out to stop the opponents even taking the ball over the half-way line. It whips up the crowd and adds to the drama of the match.

Firstly, however, we are concerned with learning about individual defence. All players must learn the correct technique for defending because in basketball every player defends, just as every player attacks, shoots and dribbles.

The technique for defending is straightforward, but to do it properly is physically tiring and mentally demanding. Basketball is a split-second game where mistakes are instantly punished by the other team scoring a basket. It is not like soccer, where if a player misses a tackle on the half-way line he still has fifty or sixty yards in which to chase his man.

Teams must therefore be able to depend on their defensive play. A team can have an 'off night' when it comes to shooting because no team, or player, will be brilliant on attack in every game. But defence must be good every time you or your team steps out onto the floor. Fail in defence and you will be punished every time the other team has the ball.

Position

CLOSE TO THE BASKET
When defending against a player who has the ball close to the basket, you must:

1. Raise one arm to try to prevent the attacker from attempting a shot; hold the other low to pressure the dribble.
2. Bend the knees so that you are posed to move quickly if the attacker tries to dribble around you. This stance gives you a low centre of gravity and the balance to spring away. The feet should be shoulder-width apart, as if you were about to sit down in a chair.
3. Watch the attacker's stomach. Do not watch the ball as this makes it easy for the attacker to fake you and ruin your balance before he moves off in another direction. By watching the stomach, the attacker's centre of gravity, you will be able to avoid being faked into a wrong move. While focusing the eyes on this area you must be aware of what else he

Fig 67   Karl Brown gets into his defensive position.

is doing by using your peripheral vision, which enables you to see round the edge of the point on which you are focusing. If the attacker brings the ball to his stomach area you can try to knock it away with a sharp upward blow; but do not overbalance.
4. Always be alert to the attacker's moves and be ready to react instantly.
5. Stand an arm's length away; if you are too close the attacker will dribble past you, too far away and he will shoot. Obviously the attacker has the ball and has the initiative, but you can take some of the initiative away by making him unsure and by trying to hurry him.

OUT OF SHOOTING RANGE
The stance is almost the same as that for defending against someone within shooting range of the basket. The difference is that the arms are extended to the side, with the palms upwards ready to hit the ball.

When the attacker moves into a dribble, the defender must go with him by sliding or shuffling.

1. Maintain the same position as before – feet shoulder-width apart, knees bent and eyes on the attacker's stomach.
2. As the attacker moves to his left, the defender pushes off his left foot and throws his right foot out to the side, then the left slides back towards the right. But the feet must never cross or come completely together; they should not get closer than about 18in (50cm), so the shuffling movement is made with many small steps.

This shuffle ensures that both feet are never off the ground, giving the defender enough grip to change direction quickly and easily. Always keep the knees bent, for balance, with the back upright. Do not bend the back.

MOVING BACKWARDS *(Figs 68 to 72)*
When the attacker dribbles towards the defender, the defender must obviously be able to move backwards. If you try to move backwards from the sliding position, when your feet are parallel to your shoulders, you will fall over! To move backwards the defender must pivot by dropping one foot back and sliding at an angle.

When you turn your feet this way, the upper body is still facing the attacker. Do not turn sideways on to the attacker, as

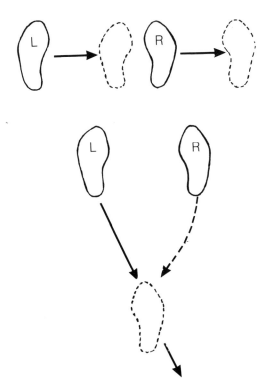

Fig 68   Sideways slide (top) and backwards slide (bottom).

keep the left hand to the side with the right hand forward at pelvis level, so the dribble cannot easily change hands.

MOVING FORWARDS

Moving forwards in the defensive stance involves the same basic technique as moving backwards. When shuffling forwards, keep one hand up to prevent the shot or pass.

Objectives

Objectives when defending the man with the ball are:

1. Halt the advance of the dribbler by forcing him away from the danger area.
2. Pressure the dribbler until he passes the ball away from the danger area.
3. Prevent the attacker from taking a good shot at the basket, that is a shot with a high chance of success. By keeping the pressure on, you will lessen the chance.
4. Pressure the attacker into making a bad pass.

this will make you a smaller obstacle and therefore easier to drive past.

If the dribbler is right-handed, try to make him move to the left by *overplaying* him; in other words, by standing towards his strong hand.

Always force the defender to dribble away from the danger area, which is, of course, the basket. So, if the attacker is in the middle of the court try to make him dribble with his weaker hand towards the sideline, therefore putting his team in a much weaker attacking position.

When the dribbler is moving to the right and using his right hand, the defender is shuffling to his left. The defender should

COACHING SESSION

Practices

MASS DEFENSIVE DRILL

Players should form three lines down the length of the court, facing the coach who is standing on the sideline, and adopt a defensive stance. On the signal the players slide in one direction, until a new direction is signalled. The players shuffle from side to side and backwards and forwards.

When the coach is sure they are all following the correct footwork he should

Fig 69 When the dribbler attacks, the defender must be able to move backwards.

Fig 70 The defender must pivot by sliding one foot back.

Fig 71 Now he is ready to slide back to cover the attacker's advance.

Fig 72 Keep the upper body facing the attacker. Do not turn sideways as this will be a smaller obstacle and easier to drive past.

Fig 73 Efthimis Redzias, the young centre from Greece, blocks the lay-up from Zuric of Croatia.

make all signals from his stomach area, to ensure that all the players are concentrating on that area. The coach should shout a few false signals to see which players are not concentrating on his stomach. For example, he might shout 'left' while his hands, held in front of his stomach, are signalling to the right.

Ensure that the players stay low, as if they were sitting on a chair. As they become more tired their legs will straighten, but this is bad technique and must not be allowed.

As the players become better, speed up the signals to sharpen their reaction time.

The time for this drill is at the coach's discretion, but the maximum should be thirty seconds as this is the maximum time you will play defence in a game. But this must be a very intense thirty-second exercise.

ZIGZAG DRILL *(Fig 74)*
In this drill, which develops individual defensive play as well as dribbling, the players divide into

67

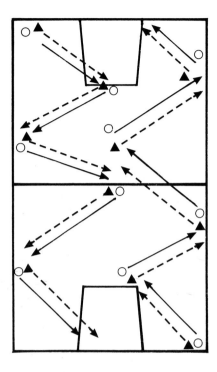

Fig 74   Zigzag drill.

When the dribbler changes hands to return up the floor the defender must drop his trailing foot back forty-five degrees and reverse the position of his hands in order to stay at arm's length from the attacker.

The defender must not cross his feet when shuffling and the attacker must use the correct hand to dribble – the left when going to the left and the right when moving to the right.

As the players improve, the dribbler speeds up, trying to beat the defender to the side of the court. If the attacker gets ahead of the defender, the defender runs ahead and then snaps back into the correct defensive stance.

The next stage in this drill is to use half of the court divided in the usual way, by the half-way line. The attacker zigzags to the basket then tries to score. The defender tries to force the dribbler away from the basket, but if the attacker gets within shooting range the defender must raise one arm to pressure the shot. If the attacker dribbles past his man, then the defender must sprint back to the basket to regain the correct defensive stance.

The last stage of this drill is to move to one-against-one on the full court, where the defender attempts to guard against the dribbler as he heads up the middle of the court by forcing him to the side. When the attacker picks up the ball to shoot, the defender moves in closer, but must not commit a foul. The defender 'windmills' his arms to try to force the attacker into making a bad shot, or one with little chance of success. However, he must not foul the attacker, or all of the defensive effort will have been wasted.

pairs sharing one ball. The court is divided into half, with a line of chairs or markers running from one basket to the other. The two groups of players face each other from opposite sides of the court.

The player with the ball attacks his particular defender by dribbling from sideline to centre line for the length of the court. The defender shuffles back and forth in front of him an arm's length away, his head level with the top of the basketball's bounce, and with the leading hand out to the side and the trailing hand between his knees ready to prevent the dribbler from changing hands.

7
Rebounding

DEFENSIVE

Basketball is a game of possession. You can score only when you have the ball. When your opponents have the ball you are defending, so it is vital to regain it. There are several ways in which you can regain possession:

1. When a team scores, the opposing team becomes the attacking side by putting the ball into play at their end of the court.
2. When one team commits a violation (i.e. failing to shoot within thirty seconds, failing to cross the half-way line within ten seconds, travelling or committing an offensive foul), possession goes to the other team.
3. When one team passes the ball out of court, possession reverts to their opponents.
4. When the defending team steals or intercepts the ball.
5. When the defending team rebounds the missed shot of the attacking team.

Rebounding, therefore, is a crucial skill in basketball, because every time your opponents miss a shot your team has the chance to take possession and, therefore, to score.

The best players in the English National League will score from about sixty to sixty-five per cent of their shots, and the best team will score, on average, from about fifty-five per cent of their shots. So, even at the top level you can see that almost half the shots are missed – and rebounded. At schools level, from beginners upwards, between sixty and ninety per cent of the shots will miss.

In this part of the game you do not have to be very tall or be able to jump very high to be a natural rebounder. It is very much a question of using the right technique to get the ball and take possession for your team. After all, ninety per cent of all rebounds are taken from below the height of the ring.

One of the most disheartening things in basketball is for the defending team to work hard to force their opponents into making a bad shot, only to see an attacker rebound a missed shot from under the basket and then score easily from close range.

Boxing or Blocking Out
(Figs 75 to 77)

The first stage in rebounding is boxing or blocking out.

Whenever you jump for a rebound you must always be between the basket and the man you are defending. If you are level with your man you have only a fifty-fifty chance of reaching the ball first.

As the shot is taken you should step towards your man and pivot so that your

Fig 75   Rebounding: as the shot is prepared the defender moves towards his man and prepares to pivot.

Fig 76   The shot is released and the defender has turned to block out the attacker and is ready to jump.

Fig 77   The defender has used his positioning to get the rebound first, leaving the attacker stranded.

backside is against his thigh, almost as if you were sitting on it. Your legs should be spread wide, just as in the defensive stance, with the elbows out and hands towards the basket ready for the rebound. By placing your rear against the attacker's thigh it will be extremely hard for him to jump. This contact also enables you to sense if the attacking player moves, so you can shuffle with him, blocking his path to the basket, without watching him. In fact, it is important not to watch your player. *Feel* where he is and concentrate on the ring of the basket, waiting to see in which direction the ball will bounce if it does not pass through the hoop.

If all five defensive players box out correctly, none of the attackers will be able to enter the area under the basket, so the ball will drop to the floor and a defender will be able to pick it up – even if he is the shortest player in the game!

When boxing out a taller player keep him as far away from the basket as possible, therefore making his height less of an advantage.

When making the step to box out a player you can either step towards the attacker then turn and block out, or block out by doing a reverse pivot towards the attacker.

You only need to box out for two or three seconds at the most, because by then the shot will have gone and the rebound will have been taken.

Boxing Out Drills

CIRCLE BOX OUT DRILL *(Fig 78)*
Players divide into pairs, with one player standing on the foul circle facing away from the basket and his partner one step away facing him. The pairs form a circle and the ball is placed on the floor in the middle.

On the whistle the attackers on the outside take one step to the right. The defender takes one step towards the attacker with his right foot, stepping through so that he ends with his backside on the attacker's thighs, and with feet shoulder-width apart, elbows out and hands up. The attackers try to reach the ball in the middle, but only by moving to the right. The defenders keep them out for a count of three and then swap positions.

For the reverse pivot box out move, the defender reverse pivots with his left foot as the attacker moves to the right. Once the

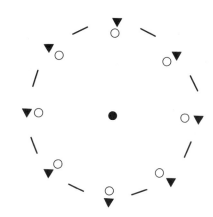

Fig 78   Circle box out drill.

players are used to the technique the attackers can move in either direction. It is important for the defenders to turn, by either stepping through or with reverse pivot, to make contact and then shuffle to prevent the attackers reaching the ball. The ball must be kept free for a count of two.

SUPERMAN DRILL
This is an excellent drill for jumping and for general fitness. A player stands slightly to the side of the basket and throws the ball against the backboard, then sprints to the other side of the key to rebound the ball before it hits the floor.

The player must move across the key in a rapid slide or shuffle without crossing the feet. The drill should be repeated for either ten rebounds or for a time limit. The ball should be caught in both hands and immediately brought down into the triple threat stance.

REBOUND PRACTICE
Players form into two lines each side of the key facing the basket. One line will consist of players who receive the outlet

71

pass from the rebounder. (An outlet pass is made by a rebounder to a team-mate immediately after catching the ball.)

The player in front of the line with the ball throws it against the backboard then runs to take the rebound. He catches the ball in two hands, lands, pivots and makes the outlet pass to the player at the front of the outlet line.

The rebounder goes to the back of the outlet line, while the player who received the ball passes to the player at the front of the rebounding line, then runs to the back of that line himself.

Fig 79   Veteran player Alan Cunningham of the Worthing Bears blocking out the taller and bigger Trevor Gordon of Manchester in the National League Play-offs at Wembley (*opposite*).

3 ON 3 REBOUND AND OUTLET *(Fig 80)*

This drill uses three attackers, three defenders and two other players who are ready to receive the outlet pass.

The coach throws the ball at the basket and the defender must box out the attackers, take a rebound, then pivot away from the basket to the side before making a safe pass, usually overhead, to the nearest outlet man.

If the attackers can take possession, either by grabbing the rebound or intercepting the outlet pass, the defenders must pay a penalty of ten press-ups or twenty sit-ups. That should make them work harder next time!

After running this drill five times, the players reverse positions.

Remember, once the rebound is taken it is vital to move the ball away from the danger area – the key – by passing the ball as wide as possible to the outlet players.

SUPER REBOUNDER DRILL

Three, four or five players stand under the basket with one ball between them. The coach throws the ball against the backboard and all the players compete for the rebound. Whoever gets the ball must try to score immediately. After the score the ball goes back to the coach, who restarts the drill.

The scoring system is one point for a rebound and two points for scoring from the rebound. Set a points target to win the drill. Players must box out, move powerfully for the rebound, gather the ball in the protected position, then jump strongly to shoot. This drill will develop players physically, and make them rebound and shoot under pressure.

OFFENSIVE

Rebounding is just as vital for the attacking team, because teams that take most of the rebounds (both defensive and offensive) usually win the games.

Anticipation is vital to offensive rebounding. Teams have patterns of attack, not only to get a good shot for one

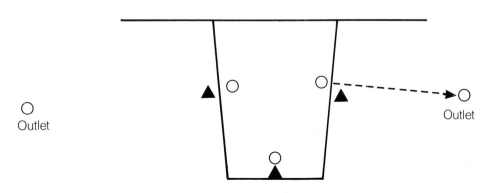

Fig 80   3 v 3 rebound and outlet.

Fig 81   Arvidas Sabonis uses his size and strength to grab the rebound from Zoran Savic of Yugoslavia.

player, but also for the non-shooting players to get into position for offensive rebounds. As the shot goes towards the basket the attacking players should be moving into offensive rebounding positions.

Watch your team-mates shooting and know who usually shoots long (with the ball bouncing out from the rear or side of the ring) and whose shots usually fall short of the target (bouncing away from the front of the ring). During a game you will use this knowledge to help you get into the best positions for rebounding.

It is best to grab an offensive rebound with two hands, then protect the ball on a strong and balanced jump as you try to score immediately. Sometimes, though, you cannot catch the ball with two hands, in which case you must go for a *tip in*, using the fingertips of one hand to knock the ball back into the basket or at least close to the ring so that a team-mate has a chance to grab the ball. This is known as 'keeping the ball alive'.

Practices

CONTINUAL TIPPING

The player throws the ball against the backboard then jumps and tips it against the backboard five more times before tipping it into the basket on the sixth go. Practise with the right hand five times, then the

left and then with both. Gradually increase the number of tips.

THROW AND TIP

Players form two lines facing the backboard, one on each side of the basket. The front player of one line throws the ball against the backboard, and as it rebounds the front player of the other line tips it into the basket. (These players then run to the back of their lines.) The third player catches the ball before it drops and throws it against the backboard, then the fourth tips it in, and so on.

2 v 1 TIPPING

Players form three lines, facing the basket. The outside lines are the attackers and the middle line the defenders. The coach throws the ball against the backboard and the first two players from the outside lines attempt to tip in while the first player from the middle line tries to stop them.

TEAM REBOUNDING PRACTICE

Players group into two teams of three, four or five depending on numbers available – in 5 v 5 there are five attackers and five defenders. The coach throws the ball at the basket, and the defenders box out and try to take the rebound while the attackers try to rebound and score. If the defenders take the rebound they make an outlet pass to the coach.

8

Fast Break Attack

Basketball is a fast-moving game incorporating many shots at the basket and lots of points scored by both teams. We saw earlier that the easiest shot to score from is the lay-up or any shot which is taken from very close to the basket. The best way to score a lay-up is to move the ball very quickly down the length of the court before the defensive team can regroup and get back to protect their basket. This style of attack is called a *fast break*, and it applies to any offence where the attackers outnumber the defenders (2 v 1, 3 v 2, 4 v 3).

The fast break is the easiest type of offensive play that you can teach a team. It is also an extremely effective means of scoring, and teams that play fast break basketball are extremely entertaining to watch – the crowds simply love them!

METHOD

The first thing you need for a fast break is the basketball. Therefore, strong defensive rebounding is absolutely essential for a fast-breaking team. Once a team has rebounded the ball they move it away from the danger area as soon as possible with an outlet pass to a team-mate who is standing between the sideline and the key area on the same side as the rebounder. The player who receives the ball is usually a guard or forward (one of the smaller and quicker players) as it is generally the taller players who take the rebounds.

Once Player 1 takes the outlet pass at the side of the court, the ball should be passed or dribbled to the middle of the court. Try to pass the ball, because that is quicker than dribbling and speed is vital to the success of the fast break.

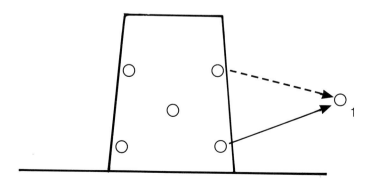

Fig 82   Fast break.

The second guard, Player 2, runs to the middle to take the pass from the outlet player. Player 2 will also be a smaller, faster player, who is a good dribbler and passer.

Once the ball is with Player 2, the player who did not get the rebound, Player 3, runs along the sideline (this is called 'running the lane' or 'running the wing'). Player 1, after passing the ball to Player 2 in the middle, runs along the other lane.

Player 2, the player with the ball in the middle of the court, dribbles quickly to the foul line. If the way ahead is completely clear he can go through for an unopposed lay-up. Normally, though, he will have to stop at the foul line because a defender is back.

Players 1 and 3 run down the sidelines, and as soon as they are level with the foul line they run directly at the basket.

Player 4 is a 'trailer', and is very important in the fast break. He comes down the floor slightly slower than the other three to make another wave of attack. He is available if the other three cannot get an easy, open shot, or as a rebounder if their shot misses.

Player 5, who took the rebound, is a second trailer. He can support the attack or offensive rebounding, or act as a 'safety man' in case the fast break fails and the other team takes possession.

Once Player 2 reaches the foul line he makes a bounce or chest pass to whichever of the players running in from the wing is in the clear. That player scores with a lay-up while the second player continues his run to make a rebound if necessary. As a further option, either of these men could pass back to Player 2, who could take a jump shot from the foul line.

This fast break should take five seconds from rebound to scoring, but, of course, in this attack there were no defenders in the way.

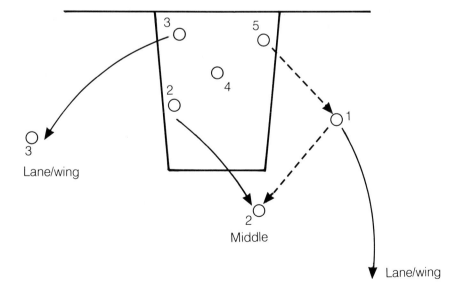

Fig 83   Outlet pass and break.

COACHING SESSION

Practices

THREE LANE PASSING

Players divide into three lines; the middle line has the ball, with the other lines on either wing. The front players in each line run down the court, passing backwards and forwards with the ball and always going through the middle man. When the middle man reaches the foul line he stops and makes a chest pass or bounce pass to one of the others cutting in from the wing. That player scores with a lay-up and the third player takes the rebound or (hopefully) collects the ball as it drops through the basket.

The need for confident, crisp passing as the players run up the court is very important, as is clear signalling from the receiver as the players use the full width of the court while passing. This drill must speed up as the players become more proficient.

HALF-COURT 2 v 1 *(Fig 84)*

The players form into three lines, two attacking and one defensive. The dribbler attacks the basket until challenged by the defender, when he passes for his team-mate to make the lay-up.

Before the dribbler passes to his team-mate he must make the defensive player commit himself. If the defender does not close in fully, then the dribbler can go through for the lay-up. The attacker without the ball should stay wide so that the defender cannot guard both players at the same time.

This exercise involves dribbling with the head up, passing under pressure and shooting under pressure.

FULL COURT 2 v 1

This is an extended version of the previous drill, with the players starting from the baseline and attacking the far basket. As they close in on the basket they must concentrate on forcing the defender to commit himself.

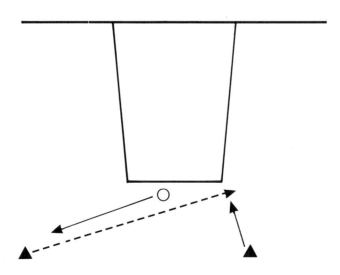

Fig 84   2 v 1 half-court.

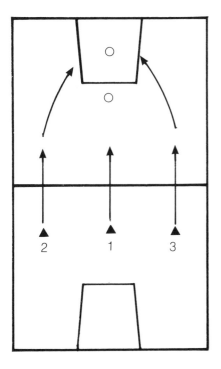

Fig 85   3 v 2 full court.

HALF-COURT 3 V 2

The players are in groups of five in this extension of the 1 v 2 half-court drill, except that now it is three players against two.

The middle man starts with the ball, with his partners at either side on the wings. When the dribbler has fully committed one defender, he passes to a free wing man. The attackers always have an advantage because the one remaining defender cannot mark both wing men, who stay wide. The wing man with the ball attacks the basket, and if he is attacked by the second defender he passes off to the other wing man, who must be unmarked. It is very important that the attacking trio stay wide, with the wing men cutting in towards the basket once they reach the foul line.

FULL COURT 3 V 2, RETURNING 2 V 1 (Figs 85 & 86)

This practice runs the same drill as for the 3 v 2 half-court, except that when the defensive team gets the ball, either by a steal or at the end line, they attack the other basket with the middle man trying to stop them, 2 v 1.

This is an excellent practice, not only for passing and shooting under pressure, but also for reacting quickly when the ball is scored or lost. The middle man must run quickly back to defend against the two former defenders, who suddenly turn into attackers.

When these three have completed their drill at the other end of the court, they become the attacking trio against

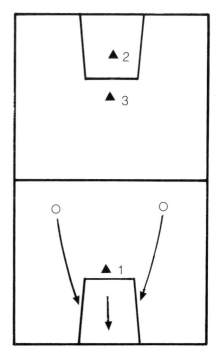

Fig 86   2 v 1 coming back. The defenders have now become attackers, with Attacker 1 running back to defend.

Fig 87   A lay-up from Predrag Danilovic for Yugoslavia. A shot typically seen
at the end of a fast break.

the two former wing men, who have been waiting at the other end to act as the next two defenders.

THREE-MAN FAST BREAK *(Fig 88)*

The players form three lines. The first person in the middle line, Player 1, throws the ball against the backboard, then jumps to take the rebound and outlets the ball to the player on the same side of the rebound, Player 2. Player 3 runs to the top of the key to receive the pass to the middle, then dribbles the ball quickly down the court to the other foul line.

The outlet man, Player 2, fills his lane, while the rebounder, Player 1, fills the other lane. The players must stay wide on the break and signal clearly to receive the pass before cutting in to score.

Remember:

1. The rebounder catches the ball in two hands, lands, pivots away from the basket and makes an outlet pass.
2. The outlet man must be in the right position, never beyond the extended foul line, because if he is too far away there is more chance of the pass being intercepted. This player must signal clearly for the outlet, then pass crisply into the middle.
3. On receiving this pass, the middle man makes a speed dribble, controlled and with head up, stopping at the other foul line to pass to the players cutting in from the wings.

Cones or markers can be used to make sure that the players run wide down the court. They must communicate with each other: the wing man shouts 'outlet' when he is ready for the pass, and the middle man shouts 'middle' when he has reached his position and wants the ball.

Once the players run this drill confidently, make life difficult for them. Put one defender on the rebounder at the start of the exercise, so that he is under pressure rebounding and when he makes the outlet pass. Also, place two defenders at the other end, waiting for the offensive trio as they attack the basket.

ELEVEN-MAN FAST BREAK *(Fig 89)*

This is a continuous practice for eleven or more players. If there are more than eleven players then the extra ones should go to the places shown in *Fig 89*.

Three players stand at half-court (Players 1, 2 and 3) and attack two defenders (Players 4 and 5). Therefore, the normal

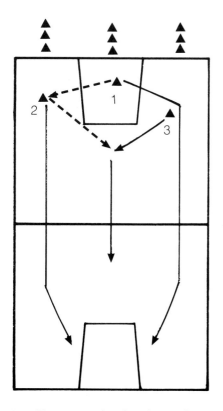

Fig 88   Three-man fast break practice.

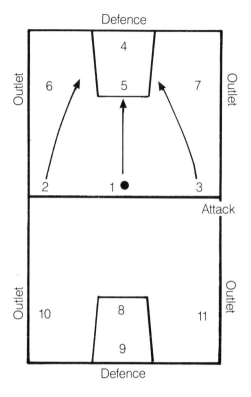

Fig 89   Eleven-man continuous fast break practice.

3 v 2 rules apply. Just one shot is allowed and all five players try to rebound the ball, with the successful player outletting to either Player 6 or 7, whoever is nearest. The outlet man dribbles the ball down the centre of the court with the rebounder filling the other lane, leaving the other four players under the basket. Two of this quartet become defenders and the other two replace the original outlets, Players 6 and 7, who are now fast breaking in the other direction.

Exactly the same happens at the other end, with one shot being attempted followed by the rebounder and the two outlet men attacking the far end.

This drill emphasizes the speed of the fast break and depends on good passing. Players should always be able to get a lay-up or make a very close-range shot at the basket. Rebounders must be aggressive – remember, there are five players trying to get the ball. Concentrate all the time as you must pass accurately.

FULL COURT FAST BREAK
This drill uses four attackers. The ball is thrown against the backboard and the nearest man, Player 1, rebounds and makes the outlet pass to Player 2, who then passes to the middle man, Player 3. Player 4 fills the other lane, and therefore Players 2, 3 and 4 are fast-breaking against three defenders, Player 1 becoming the trailer. As the trailer runs through he can receive a pass either directly from the middle man, Player 3, or from the wing men, Players 2 or 4, as he cuts to the basket. So what was initially 3 v 3 becomes 4 v 3 as the extra man joins his team-mates.

The same rules apply as in the earlier exercises – penetrate and pass. Penetrate means dribbling the ball as close in to the basket as possible to draw defenders to you. If the defenders come, then pass to the free man; if the defenders do not come to you then carry on for a lay-up or close-in shot. In this exercise, get close to the basket for a lay-up; when the shot is taken everyone except the middle man should rebound. Player 3 acts as a safety man in case the defending team takes possession.

This exercise can also be run 5 v 4, with two trailer players cutting through late, one after another against the four defenders.

In a game, most fast breaks are 2 v 1 or 3 v 2 with occasionally 4 v 3. The fast break offence can be very profitable, but it requires excellent passing, dribbling at speed and, of course, sharp shooting.

9
Basic Moves

The attacking moves in basketball are always basically the same, and the starting point is one attacker against one defender, or 1 v 1. The player with the ball tries to beat his defender either to get free to take a shot, or to draw in a second defender so that he can then pass to a free man.

Losing a Defender *(Figs 90 to 92)*

When being guarded by a player it is necessary to lose the defender for a moment so that you can receive a pass from a team-mate. Ideally, when you receive the pass you want to be within shooting range so that you are a threat. There is no danger to your opponents if you receive a pass 30ft (9m) from the basket, so they will let the ball reach you.

Attacking players like to receive the ball 15–18ft (4.5–5.5m) from the basket, but there is no point in simply running backwards and forwards across the key hoping to get a pass. Defenders will stay with you by sliding or shuffling at your side.

The first step in getting free is to move towards the defender, who will be standing between your back and the basket. The attacker places his back foot, the one nearest the basket, in front of the defender's front foot, thus stopping the defender from moving forwards in a straight line. The attacker then steps out with his other foot and signals for the ball by stretching out the arm which is furthest away from the defender. This is simple, requiring only good footwork, but is an effective way of making space. As soon as the attacker receives the ball he pivots, using the foot nearest to the basket, so that he faces the basket holding the ball in the triple threat position.

1 v 1 Moves

Once the attacker has the ball in the triple threat position he first looks to see if it is possible to pass to a team-mate who is in a better position, unmarked and closer to the basket. If it is not, the man with the ball makes a 1 v 1 move, ready to shoot straight away if the defender is in a poor position and there is a clear path to the basket. But, if the defender is well positioned, the attacker must remove his advantage by faking the defender into a bad position. The following are various fakes that can be used.

HEAD AND SHOULDER FAKE
Do not straighten the legs when preparing to make a head and shoulder fake, as you will only have to bend them again to be ready to jump or to move past the defender. The point of the fake is to make the defender straighten *his* legs, so that he cannot jump or move easily away.

To make the fake, move the ball away from the triple threat position up to head level, as if you are about to shoot. Do this well and the defender will jump to block the shot he thinks you are about to attempt. Now step by him, bouncing the ball and moving to the basket.

If the way is clear, go through for the shot. If another defender comes to you then a team-mate must be free, so find him with a pass.

CROSS-OVER STEP – FOOT FAKE

This needs constant practice but is a vital weapon to have in your armoury of moves. From the triple threat position step beside the defender as though you are going to dribble past him. As the defender moves across to stop you, bring the front foot back and place it beside the defender's other foot. If the left is the pivot foot, step with the right foot beside the defender's left foot as he moves across, then bring the right foot back and step beside the defender's right foot. This movement gives the cross-over fake its name.

Make sure you protect the ball and do not lose balance by stepping too far. Practise the cross-over step using both feet. Remember you can only move your non-pivot foot or you will be travelling.

ROCKER STEP – FOOT FAKE

From the triple threat position step forward as if dribbling past the defender, then bring your foot back to the original posi-

Fig 90 Getting free: the attacker prepares to move closer to the defender, who is marking him and trying to watch for the pass.

Fig 91 The attacker places his back foot in front of the defender's front foot, thereby stopping him from moving forwards.

Fig 92   The attacker then steps out with his other foot and signals for the ball with the arm furthest from the defender.

tion and go up for a shot. The forward step should move the defender off balance. If the defender does not react to cover your forward step then carry on past him!

As you master these attacking 1 v 1 fakes they can be combined. For example, make a rocker step then give a head and shoulder fake to get the defender jumping before you drive past him.

1 v 1 PRACTICE *(Fig 93)*
Once the footwork has been mastered, practice is needed to perfect the fakes. Begin without a defender or use a partner who will stand completely still; if you are on your own, you could use a chair.

As the footwork becomes familiar, the defender will gradually become more

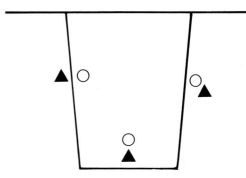

Fig 93   1 v 1 practice.

active. Attackers must start within shooting range of the basket, as they should need just one or two dribbles to score once they have passed the defender. Line up as shown in *Fig 93*.

Once a player has scored three baskets he changes roles with the defender.

1 v 1 – GETTING FREE *(Fig 94)*
Players divide into groups of three, with one passer, one attacker and a defender. The attacker breaks free from the defender, signals and receives a pass from

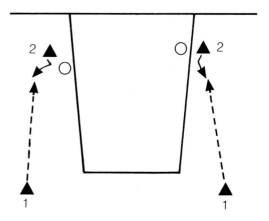

Fig 94   1 v 1 – getting free.

85

Player 1, pivots to face the basket then fakes to go 1 v 1 against the defender.

At first the attacker should use the head and shoulder fake, then the cross-over and the rocker. Once these are mastered the attacker can choose which fake to use, or combine them. This is a game-like practice as the attacker must break free to take the pass.

There should not be much dribbling – one or two dribbles at the most. Stay balanced when making the moves and when shooting. The attacker must follow his shot into the basket, to take the rebound if it misses.

2 v 2 Moves

These drills add elements to the moves which are far more likely to occur in matches. In 2 v 2 the attacker is unlikely to get a free shot at the basket after beating his defender, because the second defender will cover his path to the basket. This leaves the second attacker free for an instant, so he must move into a good attacking position to receive the pass. It is vital, therefore, that the attackers leave plenty of room between each other.

There are several 2 v 2 practices and these are listed below.

PENETRATE AND PASS *(Fig 95)*
This uses the 1 v 1 skills, with the attacker faking past his defender then driving for the basket. If the second defender covers the drive the attacker passes the ball to his partner, who is moving into a good position to score.

In *Fig 95* Attacker 1 beats Defender 1 and dribbles to the basket. Defender 2 comes across to defend Attacker 1, who passes the ball to Attacker 2, who is moving in on the basket.

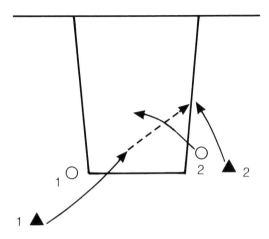

Fig 95   Penetrate and pass.

In 2 v 2 it is vital to keep the head up when dribbling to watch opponents and your partner, so you see when to pass or when to attack the basket.

GIVE AND GO *(Figs 96 & 97)*
Put simply, this means 'give' the ball then 'go' to the basket for the return pass.

In *Fig 96* Attacker 1 decides he cannot beat his defender, so he passes to Attacker 2, who is free of his defender. When Attacker 1 has passed the ball he fakes to the left, taking his defender with him, but then cuts to the right, sprinting to the basket, signalling for the ball and receiving the pass from Attacker 2 before going through to score.

This move is very effective but depends on accurate passing, a good fake and direct running. The fake involves a step or two away from the intended path, then a sudden change of direction and a sprint for the basket.

This give and go move can occur anywhere on court in order to get free, as in a lateral pass across the key *(Fig 97)*.

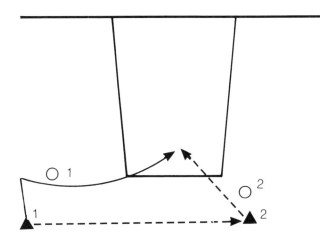

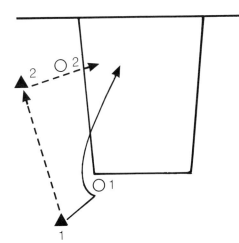

Fig 96   Give and go *(above)*.

Fig 97   Give and go.

The attackers must stay wide of each other to allow room to move.

SCREEN AND ROLL, BLOCK AND ROLL OR PICK AND ROLL

This is a fundamental attacking move used by players of all ages and abilities and in various degrees of complexity as part of their team's attacking strategy. Youngsters often find it hard to understand the concept of screen and roll, so constant practice is needed.

In the screen and roll an attacking player without the ball acts as a screen to block the path of a defender who is trying to follow another attacker.

SETTING A SCREEN *(Fig 98)*

There are some important rules for setting a screen:

1. The screening players must remain stationary once they have set the screen.
2. They must not try to make contact with, i.e. push, the defender they are screening.
3. The screening players can use only their torso to set the screen; they must not spread their arms. Therefore, contact is between the defender and the screening player's torso.

In *Fig 98* Attacker 1 has the ball and Defender 1 is defending him. Attacker 2 sets the screen to the side of the defender to stop him from moving that way.

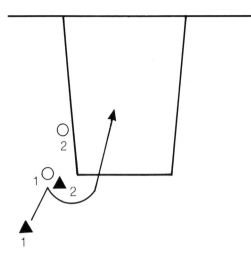

Fig 98 Setting a screen.

The screening player places his feet shoulder-width apart and crosses or folds his arms across his chest. He stands as close as possible to the defender, but must not touch him. Contact occurs only when the defender moves to try to follow his attacker, which is why the screening player protects himself by crossing his arms.

When he sees the screen has been set up, the attacker first fakes to move to the opposite side to the screen (using a foot fake or a cross-over but not dribbling the ball). As the defender follows the fake, the attacker brings his foot back around so that it is beside the screener's nearest foot. This means that there is no room for the defender to slide between the attacker and his screening team-mate. Once the attacker's foot is level with the screener's foot he dribbles past, rubbing shoulders with his team-mate to ensure that no gap is left for the defender to follow, and goes on to score.

Thus the screening player has acted as a barrier to free his team-mate by blocking the path of the defender. It is up to the man with the ball to use the screen properly by ensuring that he goes as close as possible.

PRACTICE *(Fig 99)*
Each group of three players shares one ball. Attacker 1, with the ball, is defended by Defender 1. Attacker 2 sets a screen at either side of the defender. When the screen is set, Attacker 1 fakes the opposite way then crosses back to rub shoulders with the screen, dribbling past and scoring with a lay-up.
Remember:

1. The screener must be stationary.
2. The dribbler rubs shoulders with the screener.
3. Practise screening left and right.
4. Fake before using the screen.

SETTING THE SCREEN
AND ROLLING *(Fig 100)*
When playing 2 v 2, Defender 2, who is supposed to be guarding the player setting the screen, Attacker 2, will switch his

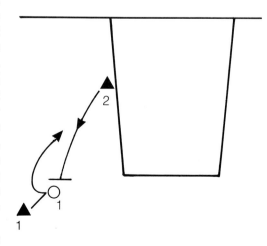

Fig 99 Practice for setting a screen.

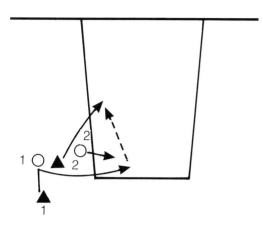

Fig 100   Setting the screen and rolling.

Fig 101   Screen and roll: the screening player folds his arms to protect himself and stands as close as possible to the defender.

Fig 102   The attacker dribbles past his screening team-mate, moving his foot as close as possible and rubbing shoulders as he passes *(above)*.

Fig 103   The screening player bars the way and prevents the defender from following his team-mate *(right)*.

Fig 104   The screening player can now roll away to receive a pass from his team-mate.

attention to the dribbler, Attacker 1, when he has used the screen successfully to get free from his defender.

In order to combat this switch of defenders, the screening man pivots in the direction of the dribbler (this is called rolling) and signals for the ball. Therefore, the dribbler now has the screener to pass to if he finds himself defended by Defender 2. The screened defender (1) is momentarily put out of the action, so the attackers now have a 2 v 1 play.

It is important that the screeners pivot, or roll, in the direction of the ball, sig-nalling to receive the pass with the hand furthest away from the defender.

DEFENDING AGAINST A SCREEN AND ROLL

As we have seen, defenders are at a disadvantage if they switch against a screen and roll, as the attackers can create a 2 v 1 situation. So the defenders should try to avoid switching.

When facing a screen and roll the defenders must communicate. The man defending the screener must shout to his team-mate that a screen is coming on the right or the left. When the defender marking the dribbler hears a screen is coming he should put his foot across the front of the screen. This way he cannot be totally blocked off and should be able to get between the dribbler and the screen. If he can do this he should beat the screen because the rules state that the screen must remain stationary, so he cannot change his position if the defender gets between him and the dribbler.

The other defender who is waiting behind the screen can help his team-mate, the one trying to defend against the dribbler. The defender behind the screen can step out into the attacker's path, slowing him up or making him go slightly wide.

The defender attempting to chase the dribbler and get through the screen must stay low and work hard to get through or around the screen.

If the defenders do have to switch (it is the responsibility of the defender marking the screener to call the 'switch'), the other defender must quickly get basket-side of the screener to prevent him rolling away, collecting a pass and going through to score.

3 v 3

This is the next step on from 2 v 2 so it becomes even more like a real game, involving both individual and team offensive skills.

PENETRATE AND PASS

The dribbler tries to beat his defender using 1 v 1 moves and then drives to the basket if he is not confronted by a second defender, or passes to an open team-mate if he is confronted. The attacker must keep his head up to see which team-mate is moving to the best position to receive the pass and score.

GIVE AND GO *(Fig 105)*

Attacker 1 passes to Attacker 3, fakes left then cuts in for the basket, signalling for

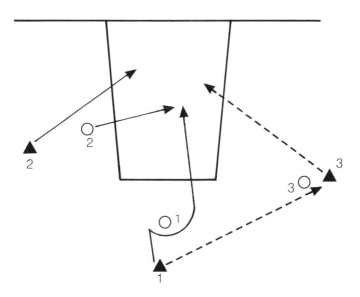

Fig 105   Give and go.

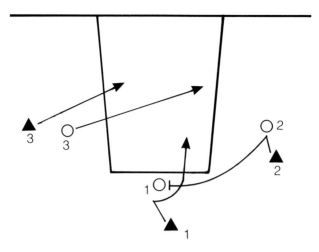

Fig 106   Screen and roll (on the ball).

the ball with the leading hand. If Attacker 1 receives the ball back and is open he should go on to score. If he has been picked up by another defender, 2, he should pass to the free man, Attacker 2, who is cutting towards the basket. It is important that Attacker 3 can make a good pass to the cutting team-mate and can also break free from his defender to receive the ball.

SCREEN AND ROLL (ON THE BALL) *(Fig 106)*
This follows the pattern for 2 v 2, where a screen is set on the defender marking the dribbler. Attacker 2 sets a screen on Defender 1. Attacker 1 fakes, then drives away from the screen to the basket. If the defenders switch, then Attacker 1 looks to pass to Attacker 2, who is rolling away after setting the original screen. If the third defender, 3, comes across to help his team-mates then Attacker 3 should be free for a pass and must cut towards the basket.

SCREEN AND ROLL (AWAY FROM THE BALL)
(Figs 107 & 108)
Attacker 1 passes to Attacker 2 then sets a screen on Defender 3 (who is defending Attacker 3). Attacker 3 fakes to the left, then cuts off the screen across the key and looks to receive the ball. Attacker 1 rolls towards the basket after setting the screen.

Attacker 2 looks to pass Attacker 3 if he is open. If the defenders have switched then Attacker 1 should be free as he rolls to the basket. Attacker 1 can also look to go 1 v 1 against Defender 2 while the screen is being set. If the pass is not on, then the players return to the starting positions to set up another 3 v 3 move.

Therefore, 3 v 3 gives players several options. Look at *Fig 107.*

1. Attacker 1 can penetrate and score or look to pass to a free man.
2. Attacker 1 can pass either to 2 or 3 then cut to the basket (give and go).
3. Attacker 1 can wait for a screen to be set on his defender by 2 or 3.
4. Attacker 1 can pass and then screen the other player (pass and screen away).

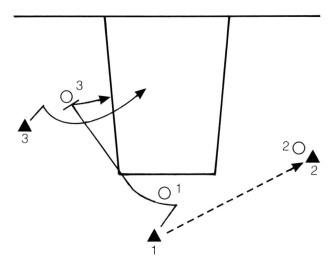

Fig 107   Screen and roll (away from the ball).

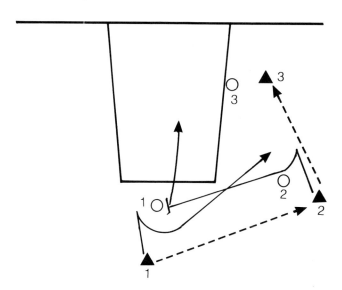

Fig 108   Game situation.

When playing 3 v 3 it becomes even more important that the players spread out to give each other room to operate; for this they should allow between 15ft and 18ft (4.5–5.5m).

An attacker must not stand still after passing the ball; always try to do something such as cutting or screening. This keeps a defender occupied and prevents him from helping his own team-mates.

93

Situations may well develop where the three attackers are on the same side, for example a point man 1, a forward 2 and a low post 3. Look at *Fig 108*. The pass goes from 1 to 2 and then to 3 at the low post. Attacker 2 sets a screen (away from the pass) on 1's defender. Attacker 1 cuts off the screen towards Attacker 3 and looks for a pass to enable him to shoot. Attacker 2 rolls down the key, after setting the screen, to receive a pass from 3 if the defenders switch on the screen. Attacker 3 can also look to go 1 v 1 against his defender from that low post position, hoping to get close to the basket to score with a power move.

COACHING SESSION

Practices for 3 v 3 should be controlled. The coach can show the options for attackers to follow the moves without facing any defenders (give and go, pass and cut, pass and screen away). The coach should then introduce only nominal defence, gradually increasing to full defence. Attackers must get free to receive the ball, face the basket and then make offensive moves.

The coach can control the 3 v 3 practice by allowing a scoring attempt only after a minimum of five passes or by insisting that a screen and roll, for example, must be used.

Apart from helping players become used to situations they will face in matches, 3 v 3 is excellent for practising both individual and team moves, occupying six players at each basket, with another three waiting to play the winners of each scrimmage.

Encourage players to play a lot of 1 v 1, 2 v 2 and 3 v 3 on half of the court while they are waiting for a larger, more formal practice and when many players want to use a few available baskets. Another advantage of 3 v 3 is that all the players get to handle the ball; with a 5 v 5 practice some players may not handle the ball so often.

10
Team Defence

Defence is extremely important in basketball where, unlike in other sports, every member of the team has to play a large part. In soccer, for example, teams are made up of attackers, defenders and midfield players; in the basketball team everybody fills these roles. This is precisely what makes the game so exciting.

We have already covered individual defence and must now put that into the context of team play. Basketball uses two main styles – zone and man-for-man. Teams must be able to play both kinds of defence.

MAN-FOR-MAN HALF-COURT

In this defence, as the name implies, each player is responsible for defending a player on the opposition. As the attackers move closer to the basket, so the defenders mark them more closely.

There are four basic principles of man-for-man defence:

1. Always get between your attacker, the ball and your basket.
2. Pressure your man as soon as he receives the ball, to deny him time to think and force him into hurried action.
3. Be ready to help a team-mate if he is beaten. There should be no such thing as 1 v 1 in team defence, because as soon as one defender is beaten another

defender should step in to pick up the ball.
4. Communicate!

Half-court defence means that you defend your man when he is in your half of the court (*Fig 109*), so it starts at the half-way line. As attackers cross this line they are picked up by their defenders.

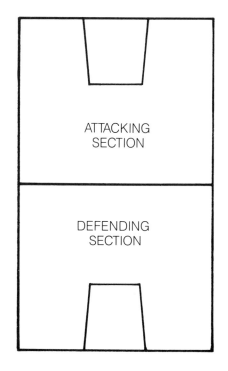

ATTACKING
SECTION

DEFENDING
SECTION

Fig 109   Half-court man-for-man defence. Half-court defence starts at the half-way line.

Practices

5 v 5 DEFENSIVE SHELL DRILL
(Figs 110 to 112)
The attackers make a horseshoe formation round the key and the defenders pick them up man-to-man. Attacker 1 has the ball.
Remember:

1. The defender marking Attacker 1 puts on the pressure using the techniques we learned in individual defence. Keep at arm's length away in the balanced defensive stance, positioned between your man and the basket. Force the attacker to his weak side: force a right-hander to the left and a left-hander to the right.
2. The defenders marking Attackers 2 and 3 must take up position between their men, the man with the ball and the basket. The defender is the third point of a triangle formed by him, his attacker and the attacker with the ball *(Fig 111)*.

The defenders are one pass away from the player with the ball, so they must also be one step away from the attacker (one step towards the ball but staying between the attacker and the basket). If the pass reaches his attacker, that defender moves in to put pressure on his man with the ball.
3. The defenders marking Attackers 4 and 5 are two passes away from the man with the ball, so they stay two steps off the players they are defending. These two steps are away from the attacker but staying in line, forming a triangle between the man he is defending, the ball and the basket *(Fig 112)*.

These defenders are the last line of defence and can therefore defend against any attacker who beats his man and dribbles towards the basket. They are also in a position to intercept passes aimed at their attackers. As the ball is passed nearer their player they move closer (e.g. one pass away – one step away).

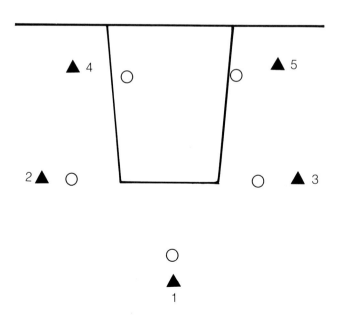

Fig 110   Defensive shell drill.

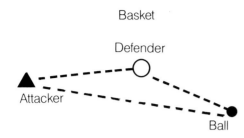

Fig 111　The defender is one pass away from the ball and therefore one step away from his attacker.

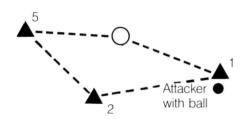

Fig 112　The defender marking 5 is two passes from the attacker with the ball, so he stays two steps away from his attacker.

STAGE 1: WORKING THE DRILL

When the coach signals, the pass is made and all five players move accordingly towards the ball. If the defender's man is one pass away from the ball then the defender is one step off his man towards the ball and the basket.

STAGE 2: COMMUNICATION

Repeating the previous drill, the defenders now communicate. The man defending the player with the ball shouts 'ball'. The nearest defender one pass away on the defender's right calls 'help right'. Similarly, the nearest defender one pass away on the defender's left shouts 'help left'. As the ball is passed around on the instructions of the coach, the defenders shout 'ball', 'help right' and 'help left'.

STAGE 3: STOPPING THE DRIBBLE
(Figs 113 & 114)

The next stage in the drill comes when the coach shouts 'dribble' after the ball has been passed between the attackers several times. On the shout, the player with the ball beats his defender (who allows him to get by). The nearest defender moves to help and the other defenders drop towards the basket, leaving the attacker who is furthest away (therefore the least dangerous) without a defender (Fig 113). Attacker 1 dribbles left; Defender 2 drops his own man to pick up Attacker 1. The other defenders all drop to defend the basket and Attacker 3 is left unguarded, furthest from the basket.

If Defender 4 is beaten on the baseline, Defender 5 moves round to pick up Attacker 4. Defender 3 quickly drops to defend Attacker 5 as he is now the most dangerous. Defenders 2 and 1 also drop the basket, leaving Attackers 2, 1 and 3 free as they are least dangerous.

When defending man-for-man, force attackers to take long shots. Do not allow them into the key area for a close-range shot or a lay-up.

STAGE 4: NO HANDS, NO LAY-UP

In this next stage of the drill the attackers can move anywhere but can score only with a lay-up. Defenders put their hands behind their backs, move their feet to help if a team-mate is beaten, and block the attacker's path to the basket with their bodies.

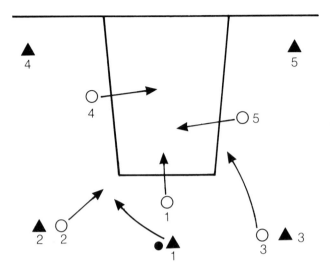

Fig 113   Stopping the dribble.

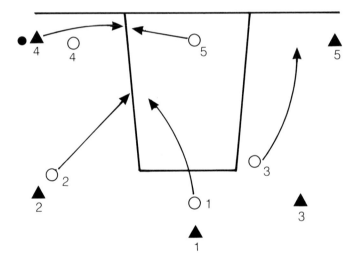

Fig 114   Stopping the dribble.

This is an excellent drill to teach positioning and footwork as the defenders are forbidden from reaching out with their hands. Ensure that the defenders communicate.

STAGE 5: 5 v 5 HALF-COURT *(Fig 115)*
The attackers aim to score with a shot inside the key, while the defenders, who are now allowed to use their arms again, force them to shoot from long range.

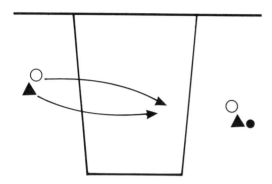

Fig 115   5 v 5 half-court, fronting the cutter.

If attackers cut across the key, defenders must stay basket-side and attempt to intercept passes to the attacker who is making for the basket. This is called *fronting the cutter*. If a pass does get through make sure it is a lob, which takes longer to travel through the air, therefore giving the defence more time to recover.

FULL COURT MAN-FOR-MAN

So far, our man-for-man defence has been half-court. Sometimes it is necessary to move this up over three-quarters of the court or even the whole court.

Coaches use a full court defence to exert even more pressure on the attacking team and hurry them into attempting poor shots or poor passes. Full court defences are also used to change the tempo and the rhythm of the game. A typical time to try a full court defence is when the defending team is behind and the game is entering the final minutes – for example, ten points down with four minutes to go.

Full court defences are called presses and they immediately pressurize the attacking team when they put the ball into play at their end of the court. The intention is to upset the other team's composure, but it is not vital to steal possession every time, although this is more likely to happen as they are forced into risky passes.

Teams who play a full court press will concede points. But the aim is to get more possession than the other team through forcing them into hurried shots, misplaced passes and violations, such as failing to move the ball over the half-way line within ten seconds.

Technique *(Figs 116 & 117)*

The positioning is similar to a half-court man-for-man with the obvious difference that the players are spread over the whole court. It is best to use the press when the ball is out of bounds and the opposing team is about to put it back into play. This gives the defenders time to pick up their men and begin exerting pressure.

Defender 1 pressurizes the player putting the ball into play by jumping up, waving his arms and trying to obscure his vision. He only has five seconds to put the ball into play, so do not allow him to have a good look at the best place for a pass. Defenders 2 and 3 are trying to deny the ball to their men. Try to force a lobbed pass, which is slow and will allow Defender 4 time to intercept. If Attackers 2 and 3 do receive the inbound pass, try to force them to receive it in the corners of the court at (a) and (b) (*Fig 116*). In these positions they can easily be trapped.

Defender 4 denies his man the ball and is also in a position to intercept lobs intended for Attackers 2 or 3. As Attacker 4 is a long way from Attacker 1, Defender 4 does not have to stay too close to him,

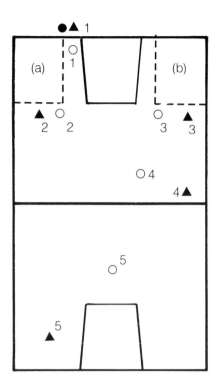

Fig 116   Full court man-for-man.

up the sideline (as in *Fig 117*), cutting him off as he turns so that the nearest man, Defender 1, comes in and traps him.

Attacker 2 receives the ball from 1. Defenders 2 and 1 trap the ball, while 3 moves towards the ball ready to intercept a pass from Attacker 2 to Attacker 1 or a longer pass to Attacker 3. Defender 4 plays in front of Attacker 4 and Defender 5 plays in front of Attacker 5.

Put simply, the idea of this press is to make the attacking team panic. If the attackers get past the front line of Defenders 1, 2 and 3, these defenders must sprint back to pick up their men again, falling into a half-court man-for-man defence (or perhaps a zone formation).

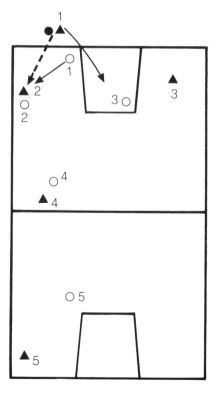

Fig 117   Full court man-for-man.

although he must always be aware of what he is doing.

Defender 5 is the last line of defence, guarding the man furthest away from the ball. He is in front of Attacker 5, as any pass would allow the defender time to intercept. Defender 5 also has an important role to play in communicating with his team-mates, telling them where the help is and where attackers are attempting to cut behind them.

Once the ball has been put into play the defending team tries to trap the ball (*Fig 117*). Two defenders mark one attacker, forcing him to make a bad pass which is either intercepted or goes out of court. The defenders make the dribbler move

Fig 118   Guard Sergei Bazarevich of Russia uses the screen set by his team-mate, centre Mikhailov.

Remember that a press is a gamble. You will not always intercept the ball. The attackers will score the occasional easy basket as they break down your press. But overall, the press should force them into poor shot selection and misplaced passes.

Always keep the pressure on the ball to make the offence hurry. Defenders must be alert and ready to switch men in order to maintain pressure. Communication is vital to prevent leaving an attacker free for a moment to attempt an unopposed shot.

Always leave the man furthest from the ball free as it would take a lob pass to reach him, giving the defender time to recover. As defenders become used to a press they begin anticipating passes and making more steals. When two defenders have formed a trap, they must keep their hands up to block the passing lanes, but should not reach in for the ball. Traps are very effective when the attacker has finished his dribble and is unable to sprint to safety.

ZONE DEFENCE

Zone defence is the alternative system to man-for-man. In this system defenders guard a particular area of the court, or zone, rather than an individual player on the other team.

Zone Defence Half-Court
(Fig 119)

There are several zone defences and I will begin with a simple 2–1–2.

Zone defences are geared to protect the area around the basket, i.e. the key. The five defenders fill the key, stopping attackers from getting inside and forcing them to shoot from outside with low

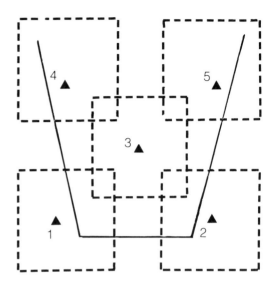

Fig 119   Zone defence, half-court.

percentage shots which have less chance of scoring. This also means that the defenders are in the best position to take rebounds from missed shots.

In a 2–1–2 the two smaller players defend at the front of the key (1 and 2); the tallest player, the post player 3, plays in the middle; and the other two taller players, the forwards 4 and 5, play at the back of the zone.

The defenders do not stand still. Playing a zone defence properly is just as tiring as a man-for-man. The defenders must stay sharp and alert, have their hands up and react as the ball is passed around the outside of the zone.

Here are the rules for defenders playing a zone:

1. The defender nearest to the attacker in possession pressures the ball at all times, denying him the space or time to make an accurate pass into the key.

2. Be big! Keep your hands up and make yourself as tall as possible to block attackers trying to get into the key.
3. Communicate at all times; tell each other where the attackers are moving.
4. When a shot is attempted, the defenders must block out the nearest man, preventing the rebound going to the offensive team.

2–3 Zone Defence *(Figs 120 to 123)*

When the ball is at the top of the zone with Attacker 1, one of the defenders, 1, defends the ball by moving out towards the three-point line; Defender 2 drops in behind him to stop a pass reaching Attacker 2 (*Fig 120*).

When the ball is passed to Attacker 4 (*Fig 121*), Defender 2 puts pressure on the ball and Defender 1 moves in front of Attacker 2 to stop the pass to the high post. Defender 4 moves closer to Attacker 5. Defender 3 stays in the key but moves in the direction of the pass and Defender 5 moves across. It is important that

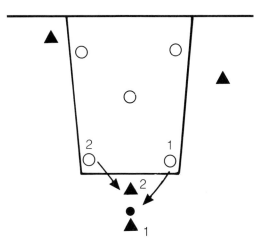

Fig 120   2–3 zone defence.

Defender 5 is aware of the player on his side, Attacker 3, and as the back man of the zone he tells Defender 3 if Attacker 3 starts to cut into the key. If Attacker 2 cuts down the key then Defender 3 must intercept any pass to that player.

If the ball goes down to Attacker 5 (*Fig 122*), then Defender 4 puts pressure on the

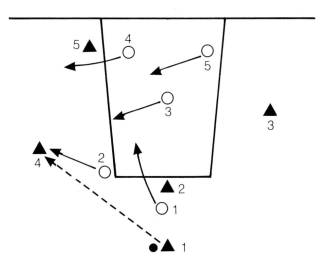

Fig 121   2–3 zone defence.

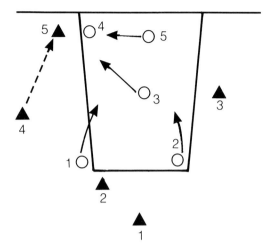

Fig 122   2–3 zone defence.

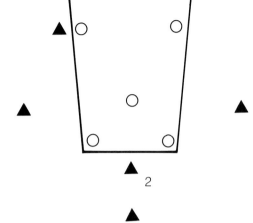

Fig 123   2–3 zone defence.

ball. Defender 3 moves down to protect the middle, 1 drops back into the key and 5 moves under the basket in case 4 gets beaten. Defender 2 drops in and is aware of the weak side of the zone and any players waiting there, such as Attacker 3. Defender 2 must tell the other defenders if Attacker 3 cuts into the key.

If the ball is successfully played into the key area, then the defenders must drop back to *clog* the middle (*Fig 123*) and force the attackers to pass the ball out of the zone again.

If the attackers have excellent long-range shooters the defenders must be aware of where they are all the time, so that they can move out from the key to pressure the shooters as soon as they get the ball. If the player at the top of the key, Attacker 1, is an accurate shooter, he must be pressured. But if he is not a shooting threat then the defenders at the front of the key do not push out on him, but drop back to prevent the attacker at the foul line, 2, from receiving the pass.

Attacking teams will concentrate on the zone's weak points: the gaps between the players. The defenders must communicate so that the gaps are covered and there is always a player marking the man with the ball.

Full Court Zone Press
(Figs 124 to 126)

A full court zone press should achieve the same as a full court man-for-man press, again with the defenders picking up an area of the court rather than an individual player.

In *Fig 124* the defenders are using a 2–2–1 full court zone press.

The defenders at the front, 1 and 2, allow the ball to be played into the court but force Attackers 2 and 3 to receive the ball close to the end line. Once the ball is passed to Attacker 2, Defender 1 tries to force him to dribble down the sideline to Defender 3. When Attacker 2 reaches the place where the areas of Defenders 1 and

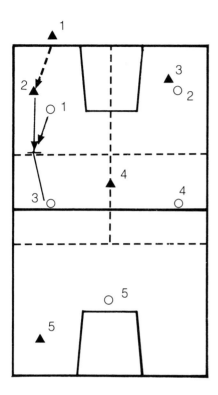

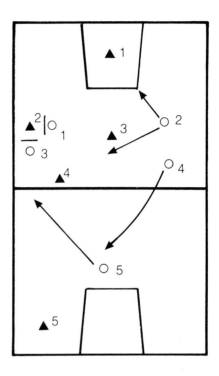

Fig 124   Full court zone press. The
dotted lines indicate the defender's
areas of responsibility.

Fig 125   Full court zone press.

3 overlap, they trap the ball. When the trap is on, Defender 2 anticipates any pass across the court. Defender 5 moves up to intercept any pass aimed over the trap and 4 rotates back to protect the basket.

In *Fig 125*, Defenders 1 and 3 form the trap, Defender 5 tries to intercept the pass to Attacker 4, Defender 2 tries to intercept passes to Attackers 1 or 3, and Defender 4 moves back to protect the basket and defend Attacker 5.

As two defenders are trapping the player with the ball there will be one free attacker. So the other free defenders must move quickly to any pass from the trapped attacker. If the pass gets through then the defenders collapse, or regroup, to a half-court defence or try to trap the ball again.

If, as in *Fig 126*, the ball comes to Attacker 2 and he dribbles down the middle of the court instead of the sideline, then Defender 2 comes across and traps him in the middle. Defenders 3 and 4 try to intercept any pass, while 5 protects the basket.

It is therefore possible to trap in any position. The aim of a good zone press is to trap the man with the ball to stop his dribble. The defender at the back must

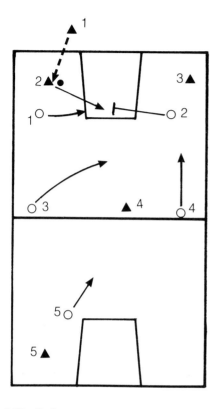

Fig 126   Full court zone press.

communicate with his team so that any attackers cutting to receive a pass can be defended. If the attackers manage to get the ball over the half-way line the defenders drop into a half-court zone or man-for-man defence depending on the instructions of the coach.

Once a team is efficient in pressing, the two defences can be combined. For example, a team can press for man-for-man full court then drop back into a half-court zone defence. If this is done well enough, the attackers can become confused and disorganized, and therefore hurried into attempting poor percentage shots or misdirected passes.

11
Team Offence

In this chapter we shall look at organized attack, or team offence, using the individual skills learned earlier. Those individual skills were developed into 2 v 2 and 3 v 3 situations (*see* Chapter 9), but now they must be put into a total team context using five players.

A team offence is an organized system of attack, devised by the coach and designed to produce a clear open shot at the basket with all the attackers working as a team and not as individuals. The other reason for having an organized attack is that all of the attackers will know where their team's shot is most likely to come from and at which stage of the offence. This will enable them to get into the right position to take offensive rebound if the shot does miss.

Once the shot is launched the taller players will move into position for the rebound while the others will retreat into 'safety' positions in case the defenders take a rebound and try to fast break in a swift counter-attack.

STYLES OF ATTACK

Because there are different styles of defence, as we have seen, there are also different styles of attack, or offence. We will look at a simple man-for-man offence, a zone offence and an attack to use against the pressing defence.

Man-for-Man Offence *(Fig 127)*

This is to be used against a man-for-man defence and is called a *motion offence*, in which the attackers will follow a series of simple rules. It is called 'motion' because all the attackers move at the same time, in an attempt to create the best shooting opportunity against the defending team.

Fig 127 shows the basic set for the motion offence. There are three attackers on the outside, with two close to the basket. Attacker 1 is the guard and best ball-handler; 2 and 3 are the forwards and good outside shooters; 4 and 5 are the tallest players and the best at scoring from close range under pressure.

This style of motion offence follows on very well from the 3 v 3 drills already discussed.

PASS AND SCREEN AWAY *(Figs 128 & 129)*
Attacker 1 passes to 3 and then sets a screen on 2, who cuts to the foul line looking for a pass from 3 so that he can shoot.

Once he has possession, Attacker 3 looks to see if he can pass to 5. If he cannot get the ball straight away he sets a screen on 4's defender, who is opposite him. Attacker 4 cuts off the screen across the key, looking to collect the pass close to the basket where he can score with a power move.

Attacker 5 rolls after setting the screen so that he can receive the ball if the two

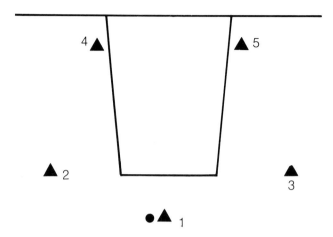

Fig 127   Man-for-man zone offence.

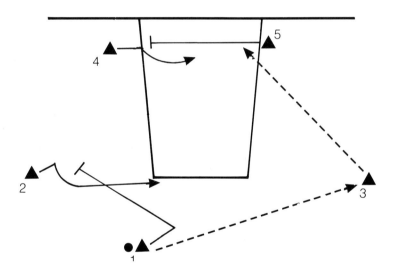

Fig 128   Pass and screen away.

defenders switch. Therefore, once 3 receives the ball he has three options:

1. He can go 1 v 1 to shoot, or penetrate to pass to the open man, usually 4 or 5.
2. He looks to pass to 5 immediately or to 4 as he cuts off the screen set by 5.
3. He can try to pass to 2, who is cutting off the screen set by 1. Attacker 2's shot will probably be from the foul line.

If nothing comes from the screens, the players can still make another pass and continue the offence (see Fig 129).

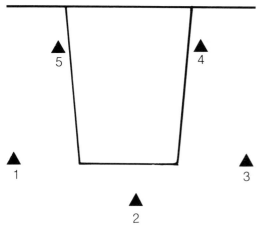

Fig 129   Pass and screen away.

It is important that the three outside players spread, so that they have room to move and set screens (look again at the 3 v 3 moves in Chapter 9). The two inside players should signal strongly for the ball and aim to receive it on the edge of the key.

PASSING TO LOW POST AND SCREENING HIGH (Figs 130 &131)

Attacker 1 passes to 3 and screens for 2, who cuts off the screen to the foul line. Attacker 3 passes to 5 at the low post position, then immediately sets a screen at the foul line for 2. Attacker 2 cuts off the screen and cuts to 5, looking for a hand-off pass so that he can shoot. Attacker 3 rolls down the key after he has screened for 2, so that if 2 does shoot then 3, 4 and 5 are all in position for the rebound. Attacker 1 meanwhile comes back out to the safety position.

Rules for the outside players:

1. Pass and move: if passing to the wing (2 and 3), cut to the basket or screen away.
2. If the pass is to the low post go and screen at the foul line.
3. One player must always fill the safety position.

PASSING TO HIGH POST (Fig 132)

Attacker 1 passes to 4, who has cut from the low post up to the high post. As soon

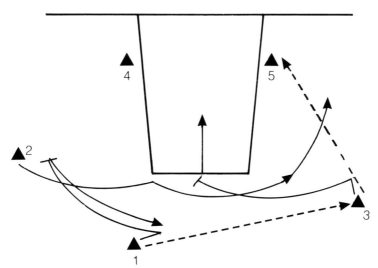

Fig 130   Passing to the low post and screening high.

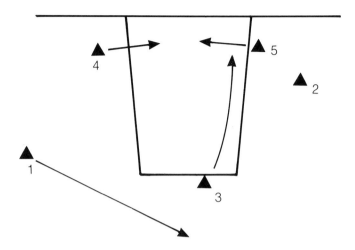

Fig 131   Passing to the low post and screening high.

as 4 receives the ball, the forward on his side, 2, cuts backdoor (i.e. along the baseline, behind the defence) to the basket and 4 looks to pass to him. If the pass is not on, Attacker 1 fakes and then cuts off 4 looking for a pass.

If Attacker 2 does not get the pass he continues out to the other forward spot and 3 moves up to the top spot previously filled by 1. If Attacker 1 does not receive the ball then he moves out to the other forward spot.

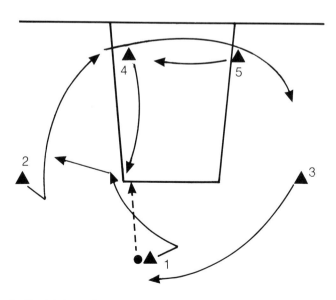

Fig 132   Passing to the high post.

Attacker 4 pivots to face the basket and looks to pass to 5, who is cutting across the key and looking for a pass under the basket. If this pass is not on, then 4 passes back out to 1, who is at the forward spot, and then moves back to the low post spot so that the offence is ready to go again.

Rules for the inside players:

1. Look for the forward cutting backdoor (either 2 or 3 depending on which side).
2. Look for a pass to 1, then cut past him to the basket.
3. Pivot and look for a pass to the other post man, who is cutting low across the key.
4. Pass the ball back out to 1 at the forward spot and move back to the low post position.

As can be seen, this is a continuous offence with certain rules for the players. All the moves end with a balanced team position, i.e. one guard, two forwards and two posts. Every time the ball is passed all the players make a move.

Practices

5 ON 0

Five attackers and no defence – what a dream! The attackers run through the offence to become used to the timing, ensuring that the players remain well spread and that the outside players look to pass to the inside players.

Whenever the ball is at the Attacker 1 spot, the post players are free to cut high and, if they receive the ball, they are then in the high post offensive position.

The point guard, Attacker 1, should always have three options:

1. Penetrate and pass, therefore making it vital that the players spread wide to give room.
2. Pass to either forward
3. Pass to the high post.

5 v 3 *(Fig 133)*

Five players attack three defenders, giving the three outside attackers (who are being defended) the chance to fake, cut

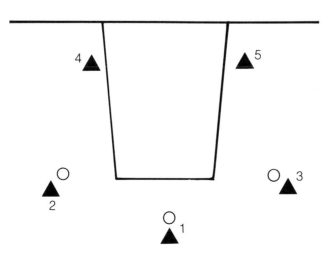

Fig 133   5 v 3 practice.

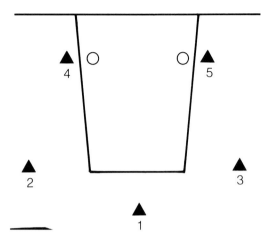

Fig 134   5 v 2 practice.

and set screens for each other. Ensure that at least one pass out of the three goes inside the key to a post player.

The outside players must not simply pass the ball around the key, they must not all be on the same side of the key and there must always be one in the safety spot. Only the outside three players can score, therefore they get used to shooting under pressure.

5 v 2 *(Fig 134)*

Five players attack two opponents, who are defending against the two inside attackers. As the offence is run, the inside attackers must concentrate on the timing of setting screens for each other, cutting high and getting free. Again, every third pass should go to the inside players. Only the inside players can score, giving them practice at shooting under pressure.

5 v 5

Five attackers face five defenders, who at first play only at half-pace to allow the attackers to get used to the offence. The defenders gradually exert more pressure on the offensive players, who must make at least five passes before attempting a shot.

This basic motion offence can form the foundation for a variety of other moves which the coach can plan and which can be brought into play by calls from the ball-handler, Attacker 1.

Zone Offence

The best way to treat a zone is to fast break quickly before the opposition has the chance to set up its defence. There are many zone defences and therefore many zone offences. Here we have a basic offence to be played against a 2–1–2 or 3–2 zone.

1–3–1 ROTATION ZONE OFFENCE *(Fig 135)*
The attackers set up with one point guard, Attacker 1; two forwards, 2 and 3; a high post, 5; and a low post or corner man, 4.

As before, 1 is the best ball-handler and usually the smallest player. Attackers 2 and 3 are the next smallest and probably the best shooters. Attacker 5 is the team's tallest player, while 4 is usually the next tallest and a better shooter than 5. He plays the edge of the key but also moves out to the corner.

When playing against a 2–1–2 or 3–2 zone, aim for the gaps between the players, which are the weak spots in the defence. So, the offence sets up in the gaps, hence the 1–3–1.

A gap in the zone defence will fall between the responsibility of the two defenders. The attacking players will exploit this while the defenders are unsure which of them should cover an offensive player.

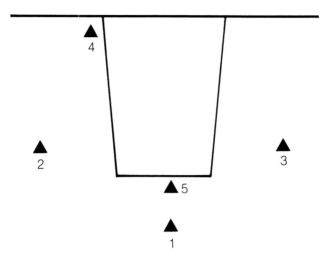

Fig 135   1–3–1 rotation offence.

Zone defences are geared to making attackers shoot from outside the key, while the offensive players are trying to get inside the key to attempt shots from closer range. To beat a zone defence it must be split apart and pulled open so that the attackers can get close in. This is done by quick, crisp passing to make the zone work very hard and move around a lot, then by penetration into the weak gaps followed by passes to free team-mates.

HIGH POST ENTRY *(Figs 136 & 137)*
Attackers 1, 2 and 3 pass the ball around the zone. When the ball is passed in to the high post, 5, he pivots to face the basket. Attacker 4 cuts in front of the rear man in the zone, looking to collect the pass and make a power move to score. At the same time, 2 and 3, the forwards, move to the gaps in case 5 passes to them for a shot from the edge of the key.

These gaps will open up because the two front players of the zone will collapse on the high post, 5, to stop him from shooting. This will leave bigger gaps behind them for 2 and 3 to step into.

It will probably not be possible to pass in to 5 immediately, but quick passing between the forwards will open up the high post area so that 5 can receive the ball either from them or from the guard.

WING/FORWARD PASS TO CORNER *(Figs 138 & 139)*
If the ball is passed to the forward on the same side as the low post, this is called the strong side. The ball is passed to 4, who has moved two or three steps to the corner away from the key, and who then receives the pass and faces the basket.

Attacker 2 cuts to the basket after passing to 4 and looks for a return pass to make a shot. As soon as 2 has cut across to the basket, 5 runs down the key to the basket, cutting to the ball-side of the middle man of the zone defence, and looking to receive the ball for a close-range shot. If 5 does not get the ball he sets up on the edge of the key and out to the other side where 3 was.

113

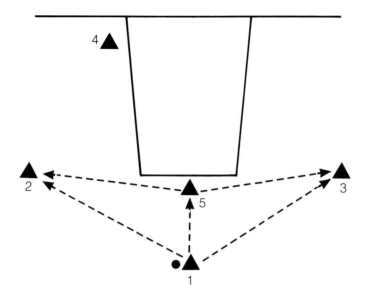

Fig 136   High post entry.

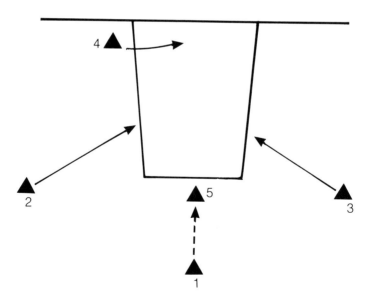

Fig 137   High post entry.

Attacker 1 rotates to fill 2's original spot, while 3 cuts to the foul line and looks for a pass to make a shot. If the ball does not come to him then he pops out to 1's original position.

If 5 does not get the ball, he returns to the high post, his original position. Therefore, the players are now back in the 1–3–1 set (*Fig 138*).

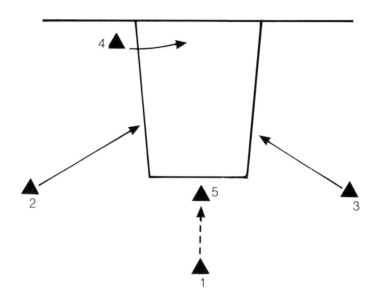

Fig 138   Wing/forward pass to the corner.

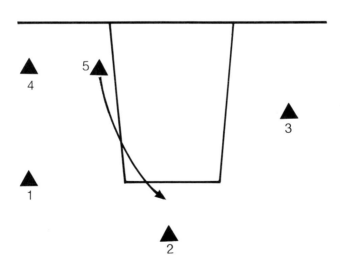

Fig 139   Wing/forward pass to the corner.

The rule for the forward when he passes to the corner is to cut through looking for a return pass, and then to run out of the opposite side to the opposite forward's spot.

The corner man, 4, pivots to face the basket and:

1. Looks to pass to 2, who is cutting.
2. Looks to pass to 5, who is cutting down the key towards the basket.
3. Looks to shoot if he is unmarked and within his shooting range.

PASS TO WEAK-SIDE FORWARD
(Figs 140 & 141)
If the ball reaches 3, the weak-side forward, he can shoot if he is unmarked within his shooting range. If not, then he looks to pass to 4, who is cutting across the zone in front of the two rear defenders.

If Attacker 4 does not receive the ball under the basket then he steps to the corner. If he gets the ball at this stage, the rotation begins again, but this time from the other side of the key.

It is not just passing and cutting that beat the zone defence. The attackers must also penetrate the gaps when the opportunities arise, opening up the zone so that the penetrating player can pass to an open team-mate.

An example of this can be seen in *Fig 141*. If a forward, 2 or 3, penetrates he looks to pass to the low post, who is stepping into the gap, as are the other forward and the high post.

1. Attacker 3 penetrates.
2. Attackers 4, 2 and 5 step into the gaps looking for a pass, a shot, or are ready to rebound 3's shot.
3. Attacker 1 is the safety man.

Therefore, to recap, the important points for a zone offence are:

1. Move the ball crisply and quickly. Passing is crucial to an effective zone offence.
2. Attackers stay in position by the gaps.
3. Attackers are ready to penetrate the gaps.

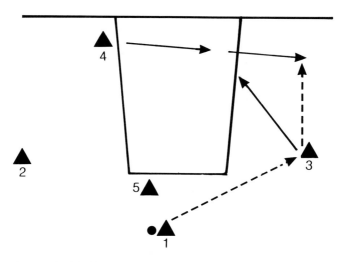

Fig 140   Pass to the weak-side forward.

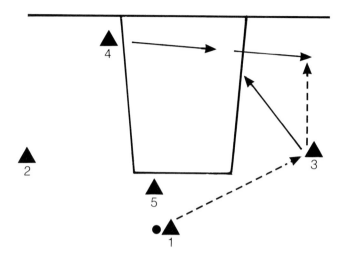

Fig 141   Weak-side forward penetrating.

4. When the shot goes up everyone except the safety man goes for the rebound.

Practices

4 V 4 PENETRATE AND PASS

Four defenders form a box, each between 8ft and 10ft (2.5m and 3m) apart. The four attackers then move into each of the gaps.

The attackers must aim to pass the ball to each other without the defenders intercepting. Attackers try to penetrate with the dribble then pass to a team-mate. They must use a low dribble so that the ball is not stolen. If the defenders collapse into the middle (sometimes called *sagging off*), then the attackers pass the ball around the outside. Attackers can cut into the middle to receive the ball then pass it out again.

Score by seeing how many interceptions the defenders can make in one minute, after which time the players change roles.

5 V 0 DRY RUN ZONE OFFENCE *(Fig 142)*

Here we have five attackers and no defence, as in the man-for-man offence drill covered earlier. This is a dry run so that the attackers can become used to the timing of their runs and the passing moves.

Ensure that the players perfect the movement and timing, that they penetrate the gaps and look for the right options.

5 V 5

Five attackers and five defenders set up in a 2–1–2 zone, with the defenders initially stationary. Again, concentrate on perfecting timing, movements and positioning.

When the attackers are confident, increase the defensive pressure to the pitch where the attackers are eventually confronting a realistic game situation zone defence.

PRESS OFFENCE *(Fig 143)*

As mentioned in Chapter 10, there are times in basketball matches when the

117

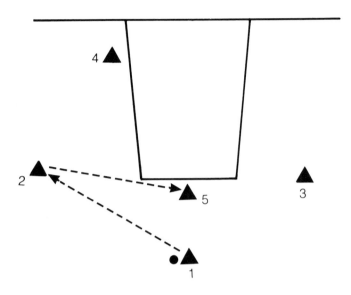

Fig 142 5 v 0 dry run zone offence *(above)*.

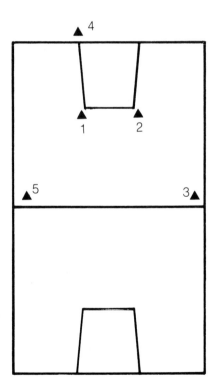

Fig 143 Offence against man-for-man or zone press (press offence).

defending team will press to try to change the rhythm of the game and upset the composure of the offensive team. When facing the press, the team with the ball must have an organized attack to beat the pressing defence whether it is a zone or a man-for-man press.

Here is the initial set-up (or 'set') for this simple press offence:

1. Attackers 1 and 2 position on the foul line, intending to get each other free for passes.
2. Attacker 4 passes the ball into play from under the basket, because most press defences are put on after a basket has been scored.
3. Attackers 3 and 5 set up in each of the corners at the half-way line.

When facing a press you must get the ball into play and up the court as soon as possible without losing possession. You

Fig 144   Excellent jump-shot by Topsakl of Turkey against Spain.

have only ten seconds to get the ball over the half-way line, and once into the other half the attackers should look to score quickly if they have a numerical advantage, as in the fast break drills practised earlier.

Initially, then, the press offence is a means of bringing the ball safely up the court under pressure, but it is also a way of scoring against a press defence. If the attacking team can 'break' the press by scoring regularly and quickly, their opponents will soon take off the press and change to a more cautious method of defence.

STAGE 1: BALL IN COURT *(Fig 145)*
Attacker 4 takes the ball out of bounds and stands one side of the basket – not underneath or the backboard may restrict the pass into court.

Attackers 1 and 2 screen for each other so that one of them can be free for the pass inbounds (i.e. the pass into court from the baseline). In *Fig 145*, 1 sets a screen for 2, who moves away to receive the pass. Attacker 1 then rolls down the key after setting the screen for 2 in case the defenders switch men.

STAGE 2: GET FREE AND PASS TO MIDDLE *(Figs 146 & 147)*
Once the ball is passed in to 2, the player opposite 2, who is at the half-court, cuts towards the ball looking to receive a pass. Once 3 receives the ball he pivots to to face the basket to be attacked, and then he looks to pass to 1, who is cutting past him down the sideline. If this pass is not on, then 3 can dribble up the floor leading a three-man fast break: 3, 1 and 5.

It is vital on a press offence to get the ball to the middle of the court where the player can pass to his left or right.

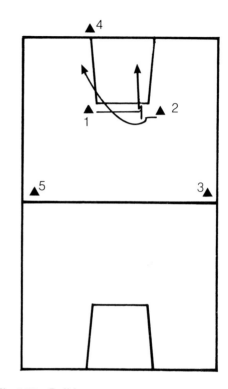

Fig 145   Ball in court.

Going back to the start of the attack, 2 could try to pass immediately to 5 if that player is open *(Fig 147)*. Then 5 would pass to 3, who holds the position in the middle of the court, and he can either pass to 1 or dribble up the court. Attacker 5 fills the other lane once the ball reaches the middle, which means the three-man fast break is still on.

If this break is run properly the three attackers, 5, 3 and 1, should be attacking the basket against two defenders, having secured the numerical advantage to make scoring easy.

STAGE 3: REVERSAL *(Fig 148)*
Attacker 2 has the ball but cannot pass to 3 or 5, so he passes back to 4, who has

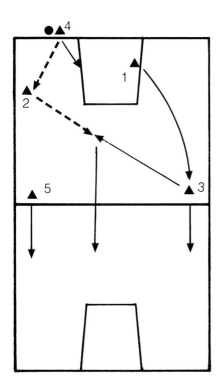

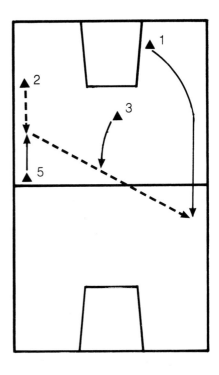

Fig 146   Getting free and passing to the middle *(above)*.

Fig 147   Getting free and passing to the middle *(top right)*.

Fig 148   Reversal *(right)*.

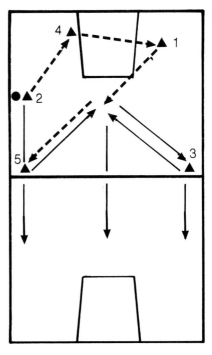

now stepped onto the court. Attacker 4 reverses the ball back to 1. Once 1 has the ball on the reversal, 5 cuts to the middle to receive the ball. When 5 gets the ball he pivots and looks to pass to 2, who is cutting. If the pass is not on, 5 dribbles up the middle of the court, again producing a three-man fast break as the counter-attack to what began as a press by the other team.

COACHING SESSION

Practices

5 V NO DEFENCE

Five attackers, without defenders, set up in their positions. Ensure that the players screen correctly and signal for passes. Cuts must be quick and direct, and preceded by a fake in the opposite direction before moving to meet the ball.

Once over the half-way line, the players attack the basket following the fast break rules covered in Chapter 8.

The coach calls out the options to be used, to make sure the players are concentrating and watching. When running a three-man break, ensure that the remaining two players follow as trailers.

5 V 3 PRESS OFFENCE *(Fig 149)*

Five attackers face three defenders who have specific areas to defend. Defender 1 can cover anywhere below the free throw line; 2 anywhere between the free throw line and the half-way line; and 3 anywhere in the attacking half-court.

The attackers run the press offence using whichever options are necessary to beat the three defenders. Concentrate on making the passes and cuts direct and fast. Penalise the attackers if the defenders steal the ball – ten press-ups!

The attackers should be able to handle

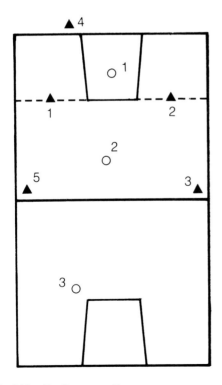

Fig 149   5 v 3 press offence.

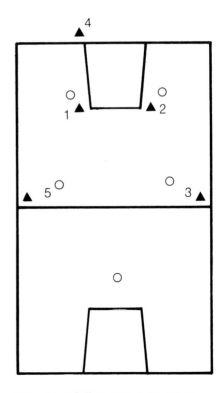

Fig 150   5 v 5 full court v zone press.

this offence easily, so concentrate on perfecting the timing, the runs and the passes.

5 v 5 FULL COURT MAN-FOR-MAN DEFENCE

Five attackers face five defenders playing full court man-for-man defence at only fifty per cent effort at first, allowing the attackers to get used to patterns of play.

Once the press offence is over the halfway line, ensure that the attackers follow the right options, namely to attack if they have the numerical advantage or to set up the man-for-man offence if they do not.

5 v 5 FULL COURT V ZONE PRESS *(Fig 150)*

Five attackers face five defenders who have set up a zone press defence. Now

the attackers have to beat a zone press with their own press offence.

The attackers must get the ball to the middle of the court, from where they can attack the defence. If it is not possible to create an easy shot immediately, the attackers then set up the appropriate offence; i.e. a zone defence or a man-for-man offence against a man-for-man defence.

The coach should always emphasize that offensive players must be quick, but must not hurry. If the easy, quick shot is not on, then be patient and set up an offence which will produce a high percentage shot at the basket.

Remember – the defenders will be trying to pressure the attackers into hurrying. Don't be rushed.

Glossary

Assist An excellent pass which enables a team-mate to score easily.

Back court The half of the court containing a team's own basket, therefore the basket they are defending. A 'back court violation' is when the team in possession passes the ball back on to their own half of the court.

Backboard The flat board, often transparent, supporting the basket.

Backdoor play When an attacking player is close to the basket but has a defender between his back and the basket, the attacker fakes to receive a pass by stepping away from the defender. He then rolls round behind the defender, going 'backdoor', and is now between the defender and the basket, free to receive a pass.

Bank shot A shot where the ball bounces into the net off the backboard.

Baseball pass A one-handed overhead pass.

Baseline The end line of the court, 4ft (1.2m) behind the backboard. A baseline drive is a powerful run along the baseline to attack the basket.

Basket The target, and the name for a score; a field basket is worth two points.

Boxing out Defensive players block opponents to prevent offensive rebounds.

Centres The tallest players in the team, also known as posts or pivots, who play around the key and must be able to score from close range and rebound strongly.

Charging foul Committed by an offensive player charging into a stationary defensive player.

'D' Abbreviation for defence. 'Tough D' means playing a determined defensive game.

Double foul Simultaneous foul by opposing players resulting in a jump ball.

Double team Two players reaching one attacker; also called a 'trap'.

Dunk One- or two-handed spectacular shot where the player takes the ball above the level of the rim and thrusts it down through the hoop. Also called a 'stuff' or a 'jam'.

Fake A feint or a dummy to deceive an opponent into making a wrong move.

Fast break Quick counter-attacking from a defensive position aimed at creating an easy scoring chance before opponents can regroup.

Field goal (or basket) Two-point or three-point scoring shot, therefore not a free throw.

Forwards Taller than guards, shorter than centres; good shooters from mid-range who play close to the basket and must be rebounders.

Free throw Penalty shots from the free-throw line, unopposed, worth one point.

Front court The half of the court containing the basket which a team attacks.

Full court press A hustling pressure defence covering the full court and not just the defending team's half.

Guards Smaller, quicker players, who should be excellent dribblers and passers and be able to shoot from long range. No 1 guard is the ball-handler, while no 2 is often the 'off guard' and a shooter.

High post The position filled by a player at the top of the key area, furthest away from the basket.

Hook shot One-handed shot with a swinging motion side-on to the basket.

Jump ball To start the game or the second half, or after a double foul, the ball is thrown up between two opposing players by an official.

Jump shot One-handed shot released at the top of the jump.

Key The key-hole shaped area extending from the baseline under the basket.

Lay-up One-handed shot against the backboard and into the basket delivered at the end of a run at the basket.

Low post Position filled at the bottom of the key area, closest to the basket, usually by the team's centre or tallest player.

Man-to-man Defensive system where a player marks an opponent, rather than covering an area of court.

Motion An offence in which the players follow a set of rules to all move at the same time in an attempt to create shooting opportunities.

One-on-one An attacker takes on one defender.

Outlet pass Starts a fast break to either sideline from a defensive rebound.

Overtime Extra five-minute periods to break a tie.

Passing lanes The areas closest to the torso which it is hardest for the defender to cover with his hands.

Playmaker The ball-handling guard.

Strong side The side of the key area into which the attacking team has passed the ball.

Three-point play When a player is fouled in the act of scoring a two-point field basket and then scores a further point from the free-throw line.

Three-point shot A basket scored from outside the 22ft (6.7m) arc.

Travelling An illegal dribble where the player fails to bounce the ball correctly.

Weak side The side of the key area where the attacking team does not have the ball.

Zone A defensive system where players cover areas of the court rather than marking individual players.

Index

OTHER TITLES IN THE SKILLS OF THE GAME SERIES

American Football	*Les Wilson*
Badminton	*Peter Roper*
Baseball and Softball	*Ian Smyth*
Canoeing	*Neil Shave*
Cricket	*Keith Andrew*
Croquet	*Bill Lamb*
Crown Green Bowls	*Harry Barratt*
Dinghy Sailing	*Rob Andrews*
Endurance Running	*Norman Brook*
Fencing	*Henry de Silva*
Fitness for Sport	*Rex Hazeldine*
Flat Green Bowls	*Gwyn John*
Flexibility for Sport	*Bob Smith*
Golf	*John Stirling*
Gymnastics	*Trevor Low*
Hockey	*John Cadman*
Judo	*Roy Inman*
Karate	*Vic Charles*
Mountain Biking	*Paul Skilbeck*
Netball	*Betty Galsworthy*
Orienteering	*Carol McNeill*
Rhythmic Gymnastics	*Jenny Bott*
Rowing	*Rosie Mayglothling*
Rugby League	*Maurice Bamford*
Rugby Union	*Barrie Corless*
Skiing	*John Shedden*
Soccer	*Tony Book*
Sprinting and Hurdling	*Peter Warden*
Squash	*Ian McKenzie*
Strength Training for Sport	*Rex Hazeldine*
Swimming	*John Verrier*
Table Tennis	*Gordon Steggall*
Tennis	*Charles Applewhaite and Bill Moss*
Trampolining	*Erika and Brian Phelps*
Triathlon	*Steve Trew*
Volleyball	*Keith Nicholls*
Water Skiing	*John West*
Windsurfing	*Ben Oakley*

Further details of titles available or in preparation can be obtained from the publishers.